IF THIS
ISN'T NICE,
WHAT IS?

third edition

IF THIS IS

N'T NICE, WHAT IS?

The graduation speeches
and other words to live by
* * *
(even more) expanded
third edition

KURT VONNEGUT

Selected and introduced by DAN WAKEFIELD

SEVEN STORIES PRESS
New York • Oakland • London

SEVEN STORIES PRESS
140 Watts Street
New York, NY 10013
www.sevenstories.com

Electronic edition published 2013, 2014, 2016, 2020
by RosettaBooks LLC, New York.
ISBN ebook edition: 978-0-79535-290-4

Library of Congress Cataloging-in-Publication Data has been applied for.
ISBN: 978-1-60980-610-1

Cover and Interior design by Stewart Cauley.

Printed in the United States

9 8 7 6 5 4 3

Publisher's Note: The art by Kurt Vonnegut in *If This Isn't Nice, What Is?*
first appeared in *Breakfast of Champions* in ad hoc fashion. Here the drawings
have been re-imagined and repurposed by our design team to accompany
the author's speeches because these particular texts and the notebook art
of these drawings seemed to us to strike up intimate conversations with
readers in similar ways. The Kurt Vonnegut Jr. Copyright Trust
agreed, and so this rather than some other more eclectic
combination of text and art is what we went with.

Chapter 1, "What to Do When You Have the Power; In the Meantime, Remember to
Skylark!," was originally published as "Up Is Better than Down" in *Wampeters Foma &*
Granfalloons by Kurt Vonnegut copyright © 1965, 1966, 1967, 1968, 1969, 1970, 1971, 1972,
1973, 1974 by Kurt Vonnegut Jr. Reprinted by permission of Dell Publishing, an imprint of
Random House, a division of Penguin Random House LLC. All rights reserved.

Chapter 2, "The Terrible Disease of Loneliness Can Be Cured!," was originally published as
"Thoughts of a Free Thinker" in *Palm Sunday: An Autobiographical Collage* by Kurt Vonnegut,
copyright © 1981 by Kurt Vonnegut. Reprinted by permission of Dell Publishing, an imprint
of Random House, a division of Penguin Random House LLC. All rights reserved.

Especially soldiers and hard-working men speak coarsely, and even our most sheltered children know that. And we all know, too, that those words really don't damage children much. They didn't damage us when we were young. It was evil deeds and lying that hurt us."

You will find no lies in Vonnegut's words of advice. He is one of the truth tellers of our time.

—Dan Wakefield

ACKNOWLEDGMENTS

The new material added to the second edition would not have been found were it not for the help of Jerome Klinkowitz, Professor of English at The University of Northern Iowa. Prof. Klinkowitz was one of the earliest appreciators of Kurt Vonnegut's work, became his trusted friend, and his many works on the author include *The Vonnegut Effect* and *Vonnegut in Fact.*

For this third edition, thanks to Christina Jarvis, Professor of English at SUNY Fredonia and Vonnegut scholar extraordinaire, for guiding the editor to important speeches included in this volume for the first time.

Thanks to Lucy Loomis and the Sturgis Library, Cape Cod, for providing Vonnegut's 1969 anti-war speech, and background articles.

Thanks to the Lilly Library at Bloomington, Indiana, home of the Vonnegut archive, for its usual aid and support.

—Dan Wakefield, editor

Contents

*new to the third edition

INTRODUCTION
Dan Wakefield

After the publication of his novel *Slaughterhouse-Five* brought him worldwide acclaim in 1969, Kurt Vonnegut became one of America's most popular graduation speakers. Even before that first of many bestsellers was published, Vonnegut had become an underground hero of the youth of the sixties who were hungry for new ways of looking at the world and alternatives to the status quo. College students were passing around dog-eared paperback copies of his earlier novels, such as *Cat's Cradle* and *The Sirens of Titan*, even before *Slaughterhouse-Five* had made him a household name. From his earliest short stories that were published in the popular

weeklies of the nineteen-fifties, including *Colliers* and *The Saturday Evening Post*, Vonnegut's work spoke to young people, and that appeal has never faded. His novels, essays, and stories are taught in colleges and high schools throughout the U.S., and as Prof. Shaun O'Connell at the University of Massachusetts in Boston has told me, "It's hard to get students to read Updike and Bellow anymore, but they still love Vonnegut."

To his own surprise and chagrin, Vonnegut was hailed as a "spokesman" of youth and a hero of the counterculture of the sixties, yet he was, ironically, a "counter-counterculture" figure. He satirized the easy promises to inner and world peace being peddled by the Maharishi Mahesh Yogi in an article for *Esquire* called "Yes, We Have No Nirvanas." As Eastern meditations such as Zen became a fad, Vonnegut maintained that we had our own Western method of achieving the same results of slowing the heartbeat and stilling the mind; it was called "reading short stories." He called this practice "Buddhist Catnaps." He was not, however, one of those adults of the era who

found nothing to admire in the youth culture. He had written that "The function of the artist is to make people like life better than before," and when asked if he'd ever seen that done he answered, "Yes, the Beatles did it."

He also loved the blues, and jazz. He wrote to a friendly literary critic that, "During my childhood in Indianapolis, local jazz musicians excited me and made me happy."

He did not believe drugs had such an effect. In one speech in this collection, he tells his audience: "I've been a coward about heroin and cocaine and LSD and so on. . . . I did smoke a joint of marijuana one time with Jerry Garcia of the Grateful Dead, just to be sociable. It didn't seem to do anything to me, one way or the other, so I never did it again."

Hardly the words of a hippie. One of the well-known hippies of that era, the writer Raymond Mungo, invited me and Vonnegut to visit the commune he started in Brattleboro, Vermont (and later wrote about in his memoir *Total Loss Farm*). He told us that one reason he and his friends wanted to start the commune and learn to "live off

the land" in a simple way was that "we want to be
the last people on earth." Vonnegut said, "Isn't that
kind of a stuck-up kind of thing to want to be?"

In the way he spoke and the way he wrote, Von-
negut was always coming up with the plain-spoken
words and phrases that people thought but didn't
say, the ideas that expressed inner feelings, that
rattled preconceptions and made you look at things
from a different angle. He was the one who pointed
out the elephant in the room, the one who saw that
the Emperor had no clothes.

That same Raymond Mungo who ushered
me and Vonnegut around his commune in 1970
emailed me recently after reading the collection of
Vonnegut's letters that I recently edited to say that
"Kurt was and remains an important writer and
one who will be read beyond all our lifetimes." A
new generation of Vonnegut fans was introduced
to his work in 2005 when he appeared on *The Daily
Show* with Jon Stewart with his last book, *A Man
Without a Country*, and teenagers are still moved
today by his stories such as *Harrison Bergeron* that
are taught in high school classes.

Vonnegut neither wrote down to his readers nor
tried to go over their heads with wisdom. He was
playful at the same time as he was profound, and
in that same style and spirit he spoke to graduating
classes. He did not speak to them as if they were a
different, lesser breed because they were young; he
disdained generation generalizations. He told one
of these graduating classes " . . . we are not mem-
bers of different generations, as unlike, as some
people would have us believe, as Eskimos and Aus-
tralian Aborigines. We are all so close to each other
in time that we should think of ourselves as broth-
ers and sisters. . . . Whenever my children complain
about the planet to me, I say 'Shut up! I just got
here myself.'" (Vonnegut had three children of his
own, and adopted four others, including his last
child, Lily, with second wife Jill Krementz.)

Popular as he was as a graduation speaker, Von-
negut never graduated from college. He left Cornell
to join the Army in World War II, and the Army
sent him to study bacteriology at Butler University
and mechanical engineering at Carnegie Tech and
the University of Tennessee, then assigned him to

the infantry and gave him a rifle. While serving
as an advanced scout for the 106th Infantry in the
Battle of the Bulge, he was captured by the Ger-
mans and sent to a prisoner of war Camp in Dres-
den, where he survived the firebombing of that city
while quartered in an underground meat locker
called Slaughterhouse-Five. When he came home
from the war he studied anthropology at the Uni-
versity of Chicago on the G.I. Bill and worked as a
reporter for the Chicago News Bureau. Although
he completed all the course work for his master's
degree, his ideas for a thesis were turned down, and
he had to move on to take a job in public relations at
General Electric. He was given an honorary degree
by the university years later, after he was famous.

"So it goes . . ."

Vonnegut's fame as a writer did not come until he
was 47 years old. Before that he struggled to support
a large family—not only his wife and their own three
children, but three children of his sister who died of
cancer at age 41, a day after her husband had been
killed when his commuter train crashed off a bridge.
The popular weekly magazines of the fifties, whose

payments for his short stories enabled Vonnegut to leave his job at General Electric, died off with the advent of television, and he had to scramble to make a living. He failed to sell a shirt company on his idea for a new kind of bow tie, had no success creating a new board game, opened a dealership for Saab automobiles when they were as yet little known in this country, and when that failed, commuted to Boston to write for an ad agency; he was turned down for a job teaching English at Cape Cod Community College, taught at a school for troubled boys, was turned down for a Guggenheim Fellowship, and through it all, kept writing. He died, in 2007, at the age of 84, still writing.

He was not about to peddle cut-rate formulas for overnight success or blue-sky bromides to young people who sought his advice.

Unlike most graduation speakers, who have a canned speech for all such occasions, simply inserting the name of a new university, Vonnegut brought something freshly minted, coming up with new ideas, new stories, new sources of wit and provocations to think about. He did, however, have certain

cherished themes that he managed to work into almost all his talks—the appreciation of teachers, the importance of noticing and acknowledging the small, sweet moments of everyday life by stopping to say, as his Uncle Alex had taught him, "If this isn't nice, what is?" His messages to graduates were not all sweetness and light by a long shot. There is always his despair at the destruction of the planet, his contempt for the politicians who get us into war from the safety of their age and position, our need for the extended families and puberty ceremonies that gave strength to past societies and whose absence plagues our own.

Vonnegut wrote that "a writer is first and foremost a teacher," and his talks to graduates always taught the lesson that underlies all his work, a lesson, bluntly uttered by a character in one of his early novels, that he passed on to fans who sought his advice: "There's only one rule I know of—Goddam it, you've got to be kind." Coming from a long line of German Freethinkers, Vonnegut was not a Christian, though he spoke of Jesus as "the greatest and most humane of human beings." In a talk he

gave at St. Clement Episcopal Church in New York
City ("Palm Sunday"), he said: "I am enchanted by
the Sermon on the Mount. Being merciful, it seems
to me, is the only good idea we have had so far. Per-
haps we will get another good idea by and by—and
then we will have two good ideas."

He served as honorary chairman of the Ameri-
can Humanist Society, and explained in one of his
talks: "We Humanists behave as honorably as we
can without any expectations of rewards or punish-
ments in the afterlife. We serve as best we can the
only abstraction with which we have any familiar-
ity, which is our community."

Vonnegut was a staunch believer in serving
one's community, wherever or whatever it might
be. Although some graduating classes will have a
"handful of celebrities" who move on to the national
stage, he pointed out that most would find them-
selves "building or strengthening your communi-
ties. Please love that destiny, if it turns out to be
yours—for communities are all that's substantial
about the world. The rest is hoop-la. And for your
footloose generation, that community could as

easily be New York City or Washington, Paris or
Houston—or Adelaide, Australia. Or Shanghai or
Kuala Lumpur."

Or it might be the city or town where you were
born and grew up. Vonnegut and I were both born
and grew up in Indianapolis, but left to go off to
college and live far away from there. Once while
we were walking down the street in New York,
Vonnegut turned to me and said, "You know, Dan,
we never had to leave home to be writers, because
there are people there just as smart and just as
dumb, just as kind and just as mean, as anywhere
else in the world." He was proud of the education he
received at Shortridge High School, where he had
worked on our school paper, *The Daily Echo*, as I did
a decade later. When asked once by an interviewer,
"Where did you get your radical ideas?" he
answered proudly and without hesitation, "The
public schools of Indianapolis."

Vonnegut took part in the communities he lived
in, serving in the Volunteer Fire Department of
Alplaus, New York, where he lived while working
for General Electric in Schenectady. When he

lived in Barnstable, on Cape Cod, Kurt and his wife Jane conducted a Great Books course for the community. (A Phi Beta Kappa from Swarthmore, Jane had him read *The Brothers Karamazov* on their honeymoon.) When he moved to New York City, he became deeply involved in the PEN Club, serving as vice president and fighting for the rights of writers around the world.

If your destiny was not to live and work in a big city or a foreign land, it was just as important and admirable, in Vonnegut's view, to serve the place where you found yourself and felt yourself fulfilled, no matter how small or obscure that place might seem to the rest of the world. When his friend Jerome Klinkowitz, a teacher and literary critic, asked his advice about moving from a small town in Iowa to a more prestigious position on the East Coast, Vonnegut wrote him, "I am certain you are highly valued and badly needed right where you are. That must be a nourishing situation. If you move East, you may find that life becomes a lot less personal." Klinkowitz heeded his advice to stay where he was, and told me years later, "It was the best advice I ever got."

In his talks, as in his books and stories and essays, Vonnegut conveys what he feels is the message many people "need desperately to receive:"

"I feel and think much as you do, care about many of the things you care about, although most people don't care about them. You are not alone."

While most of the talks here are to graduating classes, one is to the Indiana Civil Liberties Union, and another is an acceptance of the Carl Sandburg Literary Award; what he has to say in both is as relevant to young people as his words to the graduates. They convey the message that he sent to the chairman of the School Board of Drake, North Dakota, who had not only banned his novel *Slaughterhouse-Five*, but for good measure, had burned copies of it in the high school furnace:

" . . . if you were to bother to read my books, to behave as educated persons would, you would learn that they are not sexy, and do not argue in favor of wildness of any kind. They beg that people be kinder and more responsible than they often are. It is true that some of the characters speak coarsely. That is because people speak coarsely in real life.

BACCALAUREATE

A show of hands, please:
How many of you have had a teacher
at any stage of your education,
from the first grade until this day in May,
who made you happier to be alive,
prouder to be alive,
than you had previously believed
possible?
Good!
Now say the name of that teacher
to someone
sitting or standing near you.
All done?
Thank you, and drive home safely,
and God bless you all.

1.
WHAT TO DO WHEN YOU HAVE THE POWER; IN THE MEANTIME, REMEMBER TO SKYLARK!

Bennington College, Bennington, Vermont, June 1970

Vonnegut recommends "skylarking" till you have the power, and then help the old and the sick and the shy and the poor and people nobody likes.

I hope you will be very happy as members of the educated class in America. I myself have been rejected again and again.

As I said on Earth Day in New York City not long ago: It isn't often that a total pessimist is invited to speak in the springtime. I predicted that everything would become worse, and everything has become worse.

One trouble, it seems to me, is that the majority of the people who rule us, who have our money and power, are lawyers or military men. The lawyers want to talk our problems out of existence. The military men want us to find the bad guys and put bullets through their brains. These are not always the best solutions—particularly in the fields of sewage disposal and birth control.

I demand that the administration of Bennington College establish an R.O.T.C. unit here. It is imperative that we learn more about military men, since they have so much of our money and power now. It is a great mistake to drive military men from college campuses and into ghettos like Fort Benning and Fort Bragg. Make them do what they do so proudly in the midst of men and women who are educated.

When I was at Cornell University, the experiences that most stimulated my thinking were in R.O.T.C.—the manual of arms and close-order drill, and the way the officers spoke to me. Because of the military training I received at Cornell, I became a corporal at the end of World War Two.

After the war, as you know, I made a fortune as a pacifist.

You should not only have military men here, but their weapons, too—especially crowd-control weapons such as machine guns and tanks. There is a tendency among young people these days to form crowds. Young people owe it to themselves to understand how easily machine guns and tanks can control crowds.

There is a basic rule about tanks, and you should know it: The only man who ever beat a tank was John Wayne. And he was in another tank.

Now then—about machine guns: They work sort of like a garden hose, except they spray death. They should be approached with caution.

There is a lesson for all of us in machine guns and tanks: Work within the system.

How pessimistic am I, really? I was a teacher at the University of Iowa three years ago. I had hundreds of students. As nearly as I am able to determine, not one of my ex-students has seen fit to reproduce. The only other demonstration of such a widespread disinclination to reproduce took place

in Tasmania in about 1800. Native Tasmanians
gave up on babies and the love thing and all that
when white colonists, who were criminals from
England, hunted them for sport.

I used to be an optimist. This was during my
boyhood in Indianapolis. Those of you who have
seen Indianapolis will understand that it was no
easy thing to be an optimist there. It was the 500-
mile Speedway Race, and then 364 days of minia-
ture golf, and then the 500-mile Speedway Race
again.

My brother Bernard, who was nine years older,
was on his way to becoming an important scientist.
He would later discover that silver iodide particles
could precipitate certain kinds of clouds as snow or
rain. He made me very enthusiastic about science
for a while. I thought scientists were going to find
out exactly how everything worked, and then
make it work better. I fully expected that by the
time I was twenty-one, some scientist, maybe my
brother, would have taken a color photograph of
God Almighty—and sold it to *Popular Mechanics*
magazine.

Scientific truth was going to make us *so* happy and comfortable.

What actually happened when I was twenty-one was that we dropped scientific truth on Hiroshima. We killed everybody there. And I had just come home from being a prisoner of war in Dresden, which I'd seen burned to the ground. And the world was just then learning how ghastly the German extermination camps had been. So I had a heart-to-heart talk with myself.

"Hey, Corporal Vonnegut," I said to myself, "maybe you were wrong to be an optimist. Maybe pessimism is the thing."

I have been a consistent pessimist ever since, with a few exceptions. In order to persuade my wife to marry me, of course, I had to promise her that the future would be heavenly. And then I had to lie about the future again every time I thought she should have a baby. And then I had to lie to her again every time she threatened to leave me because I was too pessimistic.

I saved our marriage many times by exclaiming, "Wait! Wait! I see light at the end of the tunnel at

last!" And I wish I could bring light to *your* tunnels
today. My wife begged me to bring you light, but
there *is* no light. Everything is going to become
unimaginably worse, and never get better again.
If I lied to you about that, you would sense that I'd
lied to you, and that would be another cause for
gloom. We have enough causes for gloom.

I should like to give a motto to your class, a motto
to your entire generation. It comes from my favorite
Shakespearean play, which is *King Henry VI,
Part Three*. In the first scene of Act Two, you will
remember, Edward, Earl of March, who will later
become King Edward IV, enters with Richard, who
will later become Duke of Gloucester. They are
the Duke of York's sons. They arrive at the head
of their troops on a plain near Mortimer's Cross in
Herefordshire and immediately receive news that
their father has had his head cut off. Richard says
this, among other things, and this is the motto I give
you: "To weep is to make less the depth of grief."

Again: "To weep is to make less the depth of
grief."

It is from this same play, which has been such a

comfort to me, that we find the line, "The smallest worm will turn being trodden on." I don't have to tell you that the line is spoken by Lord Clifford in Scene One of Act Two. This is meant to be optimistic, I think, but I have to tell you that a worm can be stepped on in such a way that it can't possibly turn after you remove your foot.

I have performed this experiment for my children countless times. They are grown-ups now. They can step on worms now with no help from their Daddy. But let us pretend for a moment that worms can turn, *do* turn. And let us ask ourselves, "What would be a good, new direction for the worm of civilization to take?"

Well—it should go upward, if possible. Up is certainly better than down, or is widely believed to be. And we would be a lot safer if the Government would take its money out of science and put it into astrology and the reading of palms. I used to think that science would save us, and science certainly tried. But we can't stand any more tremendous explosions, either for or against democracy. Only in superstition is there hope. If you want to become a

friend of civilization, then become an enemy of truth
and a fanatic for harmless balderdash.

I know that millions of dollars have been spent
to produce this splendid graduating class, and that
the main hope of your teachers was, once they got
through with you, that you would no longer be super-
stitious. I'm sorry—I have to undo that now. I beg
you to believe in the most ridiculous superstition of
all: that humanity is at the center of the universe, the
fulfiller or the frustrator of the grandest dreams of
God Almighty.

If you can believe that, and make others believe it,
then there might be hope for us. Human beings might
stop treating each other like garbage, might begin
to treasure and protect each other instead. Then it
might be all right to have babies again.

Many of you will have babies anyway, if you're
anything like me. To quote the poet Schiller: "Against
stupidity the very gods themselves contend in vain."

About astrology and palmistry: They are good
because they make people feel vivid and full of pos-
sibilities. They are communism at its best. Everybody
has a birthday and almost everybody has a palm.

Take a seemingly drab person born on August
3, for instance. He's a Leo. He is proud, generous,
trusting, energetic, domineering, and authoritative!
All Leos are! He is ruled by the Sun! His gems are
the ruby and the diamond! His color is orange! His
metal is gold! This is a nobody?

His harmonious signs for business, marriage, or
companionship are Sagittarius and Aries. Anybody
here a Sagittarius or an Aries? Watch out! Here
comes destiny!

Is this lonely-looking human being really alone?
Far from it! He shares the sign of Leo with T. E.
Lawrence, Herbert Hoover, Alfred Hitchcock,
Dorothy Parker, Jacqueline Onassis, Henry Ford,
Princess Margaret, and George Bernard Shaw.
You've heard of *them*.

Look at him blush with happiness! Ask him to
show you his amazing palms! What a fantastic heart
line he has! Be on your guard, girls. Have you ever
seen a Hill of the Moon like his? Wow! This is some
human being!

Which brings us to the arts, whose purpose, in
common with astrology, is to use frauds in order to

make human beings seem more wonderful than they really are. Dancers show us human beings who move much more gracefully than human beings really move. Films and books and plays show us people talking much more entertainingly than people really talk, make paltry human enterprises seem important. Singers and musicians show us human beings making sounds far more lovely than human beings really make. Architects give us temples in which something marvelous is obviously going on. Actually, practically nothing is going on inside. And on and on.

The arts put man at the center of the universe, whether he belongs there or not. Military science, on the other hand, treats man as garbage—and his children, and his cities, too. Military science is probably right about the contemptibility of man in the vastness of the universe. Still—I deny that contemptibility, and I beg you to deny it, through the creation of appreciation of art.

A friend of mine, who is also a critic, decided to do a paper on things I'd written. He reread all my stuff, which took him about two hours and fifteen minutes, and he was exasperated when he got through. "You

know what you do?" he said. "No," I said. "What do
I do?" And he said, "You put bitter coatings on very
sweet pills."

I would like to do that now, to have the bitterness
of my pessimism melt away, leaving you with mouth-
fuls of vanilla fudge goo. But I find it harder and
harder to prepare confections of this sort—particu-
larly since our military scientists have taken to firing
at crowds of their own people. Also—I took a trip to
Biafra last January, which was a million laughs. And
this hideous war in Indochina goes on and on.

Still—I will give you what goo I have left.

It has been said many times that man's knowledge of
himself has been left far behind by his understanding
of technology, and that we can have peace and plenty
and justice only when man's knowledge of himself
catches up. This is not true. Some people hope for
great discovers in the social sciences, social equiva-
lents of F=ma and $E=mc^2$, and so on. Others think
we have to evolve, to become better monkeys with
bigger brains. We don't need more information. We
don't need bigger brains. All that is required is that we
become less selfish than we are.

We already have plenty of sound suggestions as to how we are to act if things are to become better on earth. For instance: Do unto others as you would have them do unto you. About seven hundred years ago, Thomas Aquinas had some other recommendations as to what people might do with their lives, and I do not find these made ridiculous by computers and trips to the moon and television sets. He praises the Seven Spiritual Works of Mercy, which are these:

To teach the ignorant, to counsel the doubtful, to console the sad, to reprove the sinner, to forgive the offender, to bear with the oppressive and troublesome, and to pray for us all.

He also admires the seven Corporal Works of Mercy, which are these:

To feed the hungry, to give drink to the thirty, to clothe the naked, to shelter the homeless, to visit the sick and prisoners, to ransom captives, and to bury the dead.

A great swindle of our time is the assumption that science has made religion obsolete. All science has damaged is the story of Adam and Eve and

the story of Jonah and the Whale. Everything else holds up pretty well, particularly the lessons about fairness and gentleness. People who find those lessons irrelevant in the twentieth century are simply using science as an excuse for greed and harshness.

Science has nothing to do with it, friends.

Another great swindle is that people your age are supposed to save the world. I was a graduation speaker at a little preparatory school for girls on Cape Cod, where I live. I told the girls that they were much too young to save the world and that, after they got their diplomas, they should go swimming and sailing and walking, and just fool around.

I often hear parents say to their idealistic children, "All right, you see so much that is wrong with the world—go out and *do* something about it. We're all *for* you! Go out and *save* the world."

You are four years older than those prep-school girls but still very young. You, too, have been swindled, if people have persuaded you that it is now up to you to save the world. It isn't up to you. You don't have the money and the power. You don't have the appearance of grave maturity—even though you

may be gravely mature. You don't even know how to handle dynamite. It is up to older people to save the world. You can help them.

Do not take the entire world on your shoulders. Do a certain amount of skylarking, as befits people your age. "Skylarking," incidentally, used to be a minor offense under Naval Regulations. What a charming crime. It means intolerable lack of seriousness. I would love to have had a dishonorable discharge from the United States Navy—for skylarking not just once, but again and again and again.

Many of you will undertake exceedingly serious work this summer—campaigning for humane Senators and Congressmen, helping the poor and the ignorant and the awfully old. Good. But skylark, too.

When it really is time for you to save the world, when you have some power and know your way around, when people can't mock you for looking so young, I suggest that you work for a socialist form of government. Free Enterprise is much too hard on the old and the sick and the shy and the poor and the stupid, and on people nobody likes. They just can't cut the mustard under Free Enterprise. They lack that cer-

tain something that Nelson Rockefeller, for instance, so abundantly has.

So let's divide up the wealth more fairly than we have divided it up so far. Let's make sure that everybody has enough to eat, and a decent place to live, and medical help when he needs it. Let's stop spending money on weapons, which don't work anyway, thank God, and spend money on each other. It isn't moonbeams to talk of modest plenty for all. They have it in Sweden. We can have it here. Dwight David Eisenhower once pointed out that Sweden, with its many Utopian programs, had a high rate of alcoholism and suicide and youthful unrest. Even so, I would like to see America try socialism. If we start drinking heavily and killing ourselves, and if our children start acting crazy, we can go back to good old Free Enterprise again.

2.
THE TERRIBLE DISEASE OF LONELINESS CAN BE CURED!

Hobart and William Smith Colleges, Geneva, New York,
May 26, 1974

The nuclear family doesn't provide enough companionship;
the Biafrans do it better.

Kin Hubbard was an Indianapolis newspaper
humorist. He wrote under the name of Abe Mar-
tin. My father, who was an Indianapolis architect,
knew him some. Kin Hubbard had fault to find
with commencement addresses. He thought that all
the really important information should be spread
out over four years, instead of being saved up for
one big speech at the very end.

That is an elegant joke, although nobody here

seems to be hemorrhaging with laughter. That is
just as well. I want us to be serious. I want us to
ponder seriously about commencement addresses,
to realize what it is that is withheld from students
until the very end. In the fiction game, we call a
marvelous thing withheld until the very end "the
snapper" of a tale. O. Henry probably devised more
snappers than any other writer in history. So what
is the snapper of a college education? What is the
thing that colleges hire outsiders to deliver on com-
mencement day?

The outsider is expected to answer the questions:
what is life all about, and what are new college
graduates supposed to do with it now?

<p style="text-align:center">✻</p>

This information has to be saved up until the very
end for this good reason: no responsible, truth-
loving teacher can answer those questions in class,
or even in the privacy of his office or home. No
respecter of evidence has ever found the least clue
as to what life is all about, and what people should
do with it.

Oh, there have been lots of brilliant guesses. But

honest, educated people have to identify with them as such—as guesses. What are guesses worth? Scientifically and legally, they are not worth doodley-squat. As the saying goes: "Your guess is as good as mine."

The guesses we like best, as with so many things we like best, were taught to us in childhood—by people who loved us and wished us well. We are reluctant to criticize those guesses. It is an ultimate act of rudeness to find fault with anything which is given to us in a spirit of love. So a modern, secular education is often painful. By its very nature, it invites us to question the wisdom of the ones we love.

Too bad.

<center>*</center>

I have said that one guess is as good as another, but that is only roughly so. Some guesses are crueler than others—which is to say, harder on human beings, and on other animals as well. The belief that God wants heretics burned to death is a case in point. Some guesses are more suicidal than others. The belief that a true lover of God is immune to the bites of copperheads and rattlesnakes is a case in point. Some guesses are greedier and more egocen-

tric than others. Belief in the divine right of kings
and presidents is a case in point.

Those are all discredited guesses. But it is rea-
sonable to suppose that other bad guesses are poi-
soning our lives today. A good education in skepti-
cism can help us to discover those bad guesses, and
to destroy them with mockery and contempt. Most
of them were made by honest, decent people who
had no way of knowing what we know, or what we
can find out, if we want to. We have one hell of a lot
of good information about our bodies, about our
planet, and the universe—about our past. We don't
have to guess as much as the old folks did.

※

Bertrand Russell declared that, in case he met
God, he would say to Him, "Sir, you did not give us
enough information." I would add to that, "All the
same, Sir, I'm not persuaded that we did the best we
could with the information we had. Toward the end
there, anyway we had tons of information."

Our most dismaying failure is in the use of our
knowledge of what human beings need in the way
of bodily and spiritual nourishment. And I suspect

that some of the guesses made by our ancestors are partly responsible for the starved bodies and sprits we see everywhere.

Shame on us. Less shame on our ancestors.

⁎

I myself am an ancestor, having reproduced, having written books, being fifty-one years old. I come from simpler times. When I was a boy, all a commence-ment speaker had to say was, "Go out and kill Hitler, boy. And then get married and have a lot of kids."

Some of you might still want to go looking for Hitler, in Paraguay, say. He might be there. He would be eighty-five years old now. He has prob-ably shaved off his mustache.

Some of you might go out and kill communists, but that is no longer a fashionable thing to do. And you wouldn't be killing real communists anyway. This country has fulfilled more of the requirements of the Communist Manifesto that any avowedly communist nation ever did. Maybe we're the communists.

Our politicians like to say that we have religion and the communist countries don't. I think it is just the other way around. Those countries have a

religion called Communism, and the Free World is
where sustaining religions are in very short supply.

❋

I am about to make my own ancestral guess as to
what life is all about, and what young people should
do with it. I will again issue the caveat that I am as
full of baloney as anybody, and that anybody who
says for sure what life is all about might as well
lecture on Santa Claus and the Easter Bunny, and
Tooth Fairies, as well.

I am, incidentally, the world's greatest authority on
Tooth Fairies. That is how most of my life has been
spent: in the study of Tooth Fairies. That should be
carved on my tombstone. I was the one who discov-
ered that Tooth Fairies are cannibals. Mostly, Tooth
Fairies eat Junebugs, of course. But under crowded
conditions and in an atmosphere rich in carbon mon-
oxide, Tooth Fairies eat each other, too.

And who can blame them?

❋

O.K.

What should young people do with their lives
today? Many things, obviously. But the most dar-

ing thing is to create stable communities in which the terrible disease of loneliness can be cured. Young people should also identify and encourage beliefs about life on which sane human beings almost everywhere can believe.

I suggest even here we need a new religion. If suggesting that we need a new religion is sacrilege, then the Emperor Constantine was guilty of sacrilege, and the Emperor Nero was an admirably pious man. And I want to point out that it is impossible to discard an old religion entirely. The religion of Nero survives today, determining as it does the dates and even moods of so many of our so-called Christian holidays.

Easter is a time for the renewal of life, and it always has been, apparently, even when people ate mastodon meat. Nothing is more human than to wish for renewal when springtime comes. And, out of respect for our ancestors, it is in the area of spiritual renewal that we are the most conservative and we must become less conservative.

*

What makes me think we need a new religion?

That's easy. An effective religion allows people to imagine from moment to moment what is going on and how they should behave. Christianity used to be like that. Our country is now jammed with human beings who say out loud that life is chaos to them, and that it doesn't seem to matter what anybody does next. This is worse than being seasick.

Might not we do without religion entirely? Plenty of people have tried—not in communistic countries, as I've already said, but here. A lot of people have been forced to do without it—because the old time religions they know of are too superstitious, too full of magic, too ignorant about biology and physics to harmonize with the present day.

They are told to have faith. Faith in what? Faith in faith, as nearly as I can tell. That is as detailed as many contemporary preachers care to be, except when amazing audiences of cave men. How can a preacher tell us about men and women who heard voices without raising questions about schizophrenia, a disease which we know is common in all places and all times.

＊

We know too much for old time religion; and in a way, knowledge is killing us.

The Book of Genesis is usually taken to be a story about what happened a long time ago. The beginning of it, at least, can also be read as a prophecy of what is going on right now. It may be that Eden is this planet. If that is so, then we are still in it. It may be that we, poisoned by all our knowledge, are still crawling toward the gate.

Can we spit out all our knowledge? I don't think that is possible. It is something I have often wanted to do. We are stuck with our knowledge, which has seeped into all of our tissues. We had better make the best of a bad situation, which is a wonderful human skill. We had better make use of what has poisoned us, which is knowledge.

What can we use it for?

Why don't we use it to devise realistic methods for preventing us from crawling out the gate at the Garden of Eden. We're such wonderful mechanics, maybe we can lock that gate, with us inside.

＊

It is springtime here in Paradise. There is hope in
the air!

*

If I talk about the Loud family now, will all of you
know who I mean? I don't mean everybody's noisy
neighbors, I mean a family of prosperous human
beings in California, whose last name is Loud.
They were the willing subjects last year of a televi-
sion documentary. Seemingly invisible cameramen
and sound men were able to record for all time even
the most disappointing and embarrassing moments
in their lives.

Most viewers, and the Louds themselves, claimed
to be mystified by the tin-horn tragedies and un-
funny comedies thus immortalized. I suggest to
you that the Louds were healthy Earthlings who
had everything but a religion in which they could
believe. There was nothing to tell them what they
should want, what they should shun, what they
should do next. Socrates told us that the unex-
amined life wasn't worth living. The Louds dem-
onstrated that the morally unstructured life is a
clunker, too.

Christianity could not nourish the Louds. Neither could Buddhism or the profit motive of participation in the arts, or any other nostrum on America's spiritual smorgasbord. So the Louds were dying before our eyes.

*

If my analysis is correct, then we have a formula for more such successful TV shows. Each show can feature an otherwise healthy family, from which a single life-sustaining element has been withheld. We might begin with the Watson family, which has everything but water. But no family could survive an entire television season without water, so we had better give the Watsons a diet absolutely devoid of B vitamin complex, instead.

We wouldn't tell the audience or the critics or the Watsons what was really wrong with the Watsons. We would pretend to be as puzzled as anybody about why they weren't happier with their quadra-phonic sound system and their tap dancing lessons and their Pontiac Ventura and all. We would take part in symposia with ministers and sociologists, and so forth, reaching no firm conclusions—while the Watsons slowly die of beri-beri.

A microscopic quantity of vitamins could save the Watsons. But a ton of Billy Grahams couldn't save the Louds. They know too much.

*

Now is as good a time as any to mention White House Prayer Breakfasts, I guess. I think we all know now that religion of that sort is about as nourishing to the human spirit as potassium cyanide. We have been experimenting with it. Every guinea pig died. We are up to our necks in dead guinea pigs.

The lethal ingredient in those breakfasts wasn't prayer. And it wasn't the eggs or the orange juice or the hominy grits. It was a virulent new strain of hypocrisy which did everyone in.

Talk about typhoid Mary!

*

If I have offended anyone here by talking of the need of a new religion, I apologize. I am willing to drop the word religion, and substitute three other words for it. Three other words are heartfelt moral code. We sure need such a thing, and it should be simple enough and reasonable enough for anyone

to understand. The trouble with so many of the moral codes we have inherited is that they are subject to so many interpretations. We require specialists, historians and archaeologists and linguists and so on, to tell us where this or that idea may have come from, to suggest what this or that statement might actually mean. This is good news for hypocrites, who enjoy feeling pious, no matter what they do.

If we were to try to grow recent strains of hypocrisy in the laboratory, what would we grow them in? I think they would grow like Jack's beanstalk in an homogenized mulch of ancient moral codes.

<p style="text-align:center">✳</p>

It may be that moral simplicity is not possible in modern times. It may be that simplicity and clarity can come only from a new Messiah, who may never come. We can talk about portents, if you like. I like a good portent as much as anyone. What might be the meaning of the Comet Kahoutek, which was to make us look upward, to impress us with the paltriness of our troubles, to cleanse our souls with cosmic awe. Kahoutek was a fizzle, and what might this fizzle mean?

I take it to mean that we can expect no spectacu-
lar miracles from the heavens, that the problems of
ordinary human beings will have to be solved by
ordinary human beings. The message of Kahoutek
is: "Help is not on the way. Repeat: help is not on
the way."

What about visitors from other planets, who are
supposed to be so smart? A lot of people believe
that they have already been here, and that they
taught us how to build pyramids. One that that
even the Egyptians can agree on, I think, is that we
don't need any more pyramids.

<center>*</center>

As an ordinary person, appalled as I am by the
speed with which we are wrecking our topsoil, our
drinking water, and our atmosphere, I will suggest
an idea about good and evil which might fit into a
modern and simple moral code. Evil disgusts us.
Good fills us with joy and brings a sparkle to our
eyes. That much remains the same. Might we not
go farther, though, and say that anything which
wounds the planet is evil, and anything which pre-
serves it or heals it is good. Some of you are eager

to tell me what is wrong with this, I'm sure, even though it might help to guarantee that your grandchildren had a hospitable planet to live on.

Let me be the first to say that the idea is sappy, whatever that means. I think it has something to do with being concerned about grandchildren, and the hell with them. But the worst thing about my moral code is that it invites people to have the fun of being glamorously wicked at first, which many of us feel is sexy, and then becoming almost swooningly virtuous at the end. This comes close to being the biography of Saint Augustine, and of several other famous holy men.

On a larger scale, entire nations love to blow the hell out of other nations, and then to come like angels to pass out glass eyes and artificial limbs and Hershey bars and all that, to rebuild everything, to get everything going again.

We would have to understand from the first the scientific fact that any wound we inflict on the life support systems of this planet is likely to be quite permanent. So anyone who wounded the planet, and then pretended to heal it, would simply be another

hypocrite. He would remain quite permanently an evil and therefore disgusting human being.

※

I went to a Unitarian church for a while, and it might show. The minister said one Easter Sunday that, if we listened closely to the bell on our church, we would hear that it was singing, over and over again, "No hell, no hell, no hell." No matter what we did in life, he said, we wouldn't burn throughout eternity in hell. We wouldn't even fry for ten or fifteen minutes. He was just guessing, of course.

Jimmy Breslin, on the other hand, told me one time that he sort of hankered to get back into Catholicism, because he thought there were a lot of people who deserved to roast in hell. Maybe so.

At any rate, I don't think anybody ever dreaded hell as much as most of us dread the contempt of our fellow men. Under our new and heartfelt moral code, we might be able to horrify would-be evildoers with just that: the contempt of their fellow men.

※

For that contempt to be effective, though, we would need cohesive communities, which are about as

common as bald eagles these days. And it is curious that such communities should be so rare, since human beings are genetically such gregarious creatures. They need plenty of like-minded friends and relatives almost as much as they need B complex vitamins and a heart-felt moral code.

I know Sargent Shriver slightly. When he was campaigning for Vice President, he asked me if I had any ideas. You remember there was plenty of money around, but, as far as ideas went, both parties were in a state of destitution. So I told him, and I am afraid he didn't listen, that the number one American killer wasn't cardio-vascular disease, but loneliness. I told him that he and McGovern could swamp the Republicans if they would promise to cure that disease. I even gave him a slogan to put on buttons and flags and billboards: "Lonesome no more!"

The rest is history.

*

I was in Biafra several years ago, at the bitter end of the Nigerian Civil War. The Biafrans had nothing to eat, you'll remember. They were blockaded,

so no food got in. They had almost nothing to fight with, expect for some Mauser rifles which were a good deal older than I was. And still they fought on. They had no recruiting program. There was no scheme for the relief of refugees, and needed none. The government did nothing to look out after the old, the sick, either. Biafra, for the short time it lasted, could be admired simultaneously by both anarchists and conservatives.

The people could look out for each other, without any help from the central government, because every Biafran was a member of an extended family. He had hundreds of relatives he knew by name and reputation. Some Biafrans had thousands of relatives or more.

Those families took care of their own wounded, their own lunatics, their own refugees. They shared equally whatever they had. The government didn't have to send a policeman to make sure the food was divided fairly. When the government needed new soldiers, it told each family how many recruits it was expected to send. The family decided then who was to go.

And this admirable scheme was far from being an invention by the Biafrans. They were simply continuing to live as human beings have lived until recently.

I have seen the past, and it works.

We should return to extended families as quickly as we can, and be lonesome no more, lonesome no more.

Some of you will become leaders, although that is now thought to be a grungy destiny. Nobody wants to be Papa any more. If you do have to lead, you may imagine that your mission is to help us find an amazing future. You should consider the possibility that you could serve the people better if you were to lead them intelligently and imaginatively back to some of the more humane and comforting institutions of the past.

It seems certain that you will face plenty of social unrest in the future, and demands will continue to be made for economic justice. You will be very shrewd leaders indeed if you recognize that the people are in fact crying out not so much for money as for relief from loneliness.

*

Let me beguile you just a little bit more about extended families. Let us talk about divorce, and

that fact that one out of every three of us here has
been or will be divorced. When we do it, we will
very likely wrangle and wail and weep formlessly
about money and sex, about treachery, about out-
growing one another, about how close love is to
hate, and so on. Nobody ever gets anywhere near
close to the truth, which is this: the nuclear family
doesn't provide nearly enough companionship.

I am going to write a play about the breakup of
a marriage, and at the end of the play I am going to
have a character say what people should say to each
other in real life at the end of a marriage: "I'm sorry.
You, being human, need a hundred different affec-
tionate and like-minded companions. I'm only one
person. I've tried, but I could never be a hundred
people to you. You've tried, but you could never be
a hundred people to me. Too bad. Goodbye."

Let's talk about the incompatibility between parents
and children, which happens often merely because
of genetic rotten luck. In a nuclear family, children
and parents can be locked in hellish close combat for
twenty-one years and more. In an extended family, a
child has scores of other homes to go to in search of

love and understanding. He need not stay home and
torture his parents, and he need not starve for love.

In an extended family, anybody can bug out of his
own house for months, and still be among relatives.
Nobody has to go on a hopeless quest for friendly
strangers, which is what most Americans have to do.

Massage parlors come to mind—bus stations and
bars.

<p style="text-align:center">*</p>

You graduates here are leaving an artificial
extended family now. Even if you hated it here, you
will find a nuclear family to be a very poor substi-
tute for what you had here. As for those of us who
have come to praise you for having graduated: we
have fled here from loneliness, to be part of an arti-
ficial extended family for just a little while.

And what we will all be seeking when we
decamp, and for the rest of our lives, will be large,
stable communities of like-minded people, which
is to say relatives. They no longer exist. The lack of
them is not only the main cause, but probably the
only cause of our shapeless discontent in the midst
of such prosperity.

We thought we could do without tribes and clans.
Well, we can't.

There was a time when I was avid to invent new
religions and social orders. It has now penetrated
my skull that such schemes will not work without
the support of huge gruesome police forces and
prison systems, unless they are allowed to invent
themselves. The Emperor Constantine did not,
after all, invent anything. He had many religions
to choose from. He selected Christianity because it
seemed to him to be most refreshing.

Hitler and Lenin and some others have also tried
to refresh their people with ideas that had been
around a while. They chose abominably, as we
know. It matters what we choose. And history and
the deteriorating physical and moral environments
are now telling us what we would rather not hear,
what we would rather our children or grandchil-
dren would hear: It is our turn to choose.

❈

At least we do not have to choose between vari-
ous theories of magic, of ways to manipulate God
and the Devil and whatever, which is what our

ancestors had to do. We no longer believe that God causes earthquakes and crop failures and plagues when he gets mad at us. We no longer imagine that he can be cooled off by sacrifices and festivals and gifts. I am so glad we don't have to think up presents for Him anymore. What's the perfect gift for someone who has everything?

The perfect gift for somebody who has everything, of course, is nothing. Any gifts we have should be given to creatures right on the surface of the planet, it seems to me. If God gets angry about that, we can call in the Massachusetts Institute of Technology. There's a very good chance they can calm him down.

<div align="center">❊</div>

The new moral code we choose may already have martyrs. It is difficult to spot such things. One corpse tends to look pretty much like another one— until the historians sort them out with the benefit of hindsight.

We shall see what we shall see.

<div align="center">❊</div>

For two-thirds of my life I have been a pessimist. I am astonished to find myself an optimist now.

I feel now that I have been underestimating the intelligence and resourcefulness of man. I honestly thought that we were so stupid that we would continue to tear the planet to pieces, to sell it to each other, to burn it up. I've never expected thermonuclear war. What seemed certain to me was that we would simply gobble up the planet out of boredom and greed, not in centuries, but in ten or twenty years.

Kilgore Trout wrote a science-fiction story called the Planet Gobblers one time. It was about us, and we were the terrors of the universe. We were sort of inter-planetary termites. We would arrive on a planet, gobble it up, and die. But before we died, we always sent out space ships to start tiny colonies elsewhere. We were a disease, since it was not necessary to inhabit planets with such horrifying destructiveness. It is easy to take good care of a planet.

Our grandchildren will surely think of us as Planet Gobblers. Poorer nations than America think of America as a Planet Gobbler right now. But that is going to change. There is welling up

within us a willingness to say, "No, thank you," to
our factories. We were once maniacs for posses-
sions, imagining that they would somehow moder-
ate or somehow compensate us for our loneliness.

The experiment has been tried in this most afflu-
ent nation in all of human history. Possessions help
a little, but not as much as the advertisers said they
were supposed to, and we are now aware of how
permanently the manufacture of some of those
products hurts the planet.

So there is a willingness to do without them.

＊

There is a willingness to do whatever we need to
do in order to have life on the planet go on for a
long, long time. I didn't used to think that. And
that willingness has to be a religious enthusiasm,
since it celebrates life, since it calls for meaningful
sacrifices.

This is bad news for business, as we know it
now. It should be thrilling news for persons who
love to teach and lead. And thank God we have
solid information in the place of superstition!
Thank God we are beginning to dream of human

communities which are designed to harmonize with what human beings really need and are.

And now I say you have just heard an atheist thank God not once, but twice.

God Bless the class of 1974.

3.
LET THE KILLING STOP

Barnstable High School, Barnstable, Massachusetts,
October 23, 1969

"Vietnam is not a football game. It's a slaughterhouse.
They're keeping the score with bodies."

After a Vietnam Moratorium Day peace march in
Hyannis, Cape Cod, Vonnegut spoke to eight hundred
people that night who were crowded into the high school at
Barnstable, where he lived with his wife and six children.
His overnight best-selling novel Slaughterhouse-Five,
inspired by his experience surviving the fire-bombing
of Dresden as a prisoner of war, had been published the
previous March.

This is no time for a long and glorious speech.

Our message is in the fact of our being here.

Our presence says all there is to say: "Let the killing stop."

There will be no cheering.

We have nothing to celebrate.

We are here because our leaders have made mistakes which have had ghastly consequences—cripplings and death and corruption. We are here to help our leaders make sure that the tragedy will not go on and on and on and on—and that the final solution will not be genocide or a hydrogen bomb.

We are here to help.

Our President has had the best advice of the honorable military men, who are brave.

Let him hear from honorable civilians, as well. We're brave, too.

❊

No speaker can lift your hearts tonight, for no speaker can say the only word you want to hear: "There is peace in Vietnam."

It might be possible to thrill some of you with a speech full of hatred for the brass hats and for the corporations who are making big money out of this war.

But hatred has no place here tonight.

This is a magic night.

Millions of Americans are gathered in meetings

like this all over the country—and the mood of this
night is love.

The loving thing we are saying by being here is
this: "Let the killing stop."

Those who scorn us for our eminently Christian
words say this: "Let the killing go on. You don't
know what the military knows," they say. Well—we
know as much about death as the military does.
You don't have to go to West Point or Fort Benning
to learn about death. We're against it, not for it.

Let the killing stop.

✤

What about the South Vietnamese who will be mur-
dered by the North Vietnamese, if we withdraw?

We'll help them get out, too.

They can come over here, and have their first
taste of freedom.

✤

I do not propose to retell the shabby history of this
war. It was a civil war. We weren't attacked there.
We chose sides in the civil war, and we attacked. It
was a horrible mistake—resulting in thousands and
thousands of deaths for nothing.

We are here to tell our President that we will not be ashamed if he admits it was a mistake. We can stand the resulting embarrassment. What is intolerable to us is that the mistake should go on and on and on. We are here to save lives. We are here to save our honor, too. We are here to prevent a victory through genocide.

❈

Every country makes mistakes. Only profoundly free and honorable nations can admit they make them. Dictatorships never do. In Vietnam we have made a lulu of a mistake. Tonight we are telling the world: "We have made a lulu."

This will make the communists everywhere gloat. All sorts of things make them gloat. We have a few gloaters on our side, too. Well—tonight let all the gloaters gloat. They can have a perfect orgy of gloating tonight, and I won't care.

❈

Speaking of Lulus: Hanoi certainly made one when they officially praised this moratorium. Thanks a lot, Hanoi. Well—they're people too. Everybody makes lulus.

*

Hanoi. There's a sinister word. Hanoi does this.
Hanoi does that. Hanoi. At other times there have
been other sinister words like that: Rome, Berlin,
Tokyo. And it wasn't silly of Americans in other
times to speak of these cities with dread. There
were many people in them who were turned into
maniacs by war. They aren't maniacs anymore. We
didn't teach them how to act nice. It was simply
that the killing stopped. We have a right to shud-
der now when we speak the word: Hanoi. Ghoulish
things have happened to innocent persons in Viet-
nam—at the instigation of Hanoi. I don't believe a
lot of things our Government says about the war. I
do believe that thousands of civilians were massa-
cred at Hue—in keeping with orders from Hanoi. I
believe, too, that we bomb blindly, that our Green
Berets murdered a citizen of another country in
cold blood. I believe that we torture prisoners, and
so does Hanoi.

And on and on.

War turns everybody into maniacs.

In other parts of the world, "Washington" is a

sinister word, and properly so. So let the killing
stop, in order that the maniacs on both sides can
become nice human beings again.

I would like to say something about the body
counts.

This is how we measure victory, since we have
no other way of doing so. We announce each day:
"So and so many communists killed." Perhaps the
other side counts the bodies of our young men and
announces, so and so many capitalists killed.

The dead soldiers were barely out of childhood.

They're dead capitalists or communists now.

How ridiculous and untrue—and gruesome.

※

Let the killing stop. We live in rural communities,
and are consequently privileged to see acts of unself-
ishness and bravery almost every day. I am speaking
of our volunteer firemen and our rescue squads. The
moment the siren blows, they come! They live in the
tradition of the American minute men, and God bless
them for that. In the past, Americans have proudly
responded almost as quickly to calls of war. This is
properly called patriotism. Some Americans believe

that this is the ONLY form of patriotism. What does the patriot do? He goes to war.

This is nuts.

There are all kinds of things a patriot can do. We're here with the patriotic purpose of saving lives. If this is treason, make the most of it.

I hope nobody believes that we are supporting a democratic regime in Vietnam. We are supporting dictators who are supposedly on our team. They don't call themselves communists, but everything that is vile about communist leaders is vile about them, too. Some team we've got.

Well—whatever team you belong to, you fight for, right? We want our team to win. That's great thinking for high school, particularly if you're a football coach. At Nauset, at Barnstable, at Provincetown, at Bourne . . . And so much of the fighting talk I hear about Vietnam sounds exactly the way people talk about football games . . .

You fight!

You win!

My God—Vietnam is no football game. It's a slaughterhouse!

They're keeping the score with bodies!
It's turning us all into maniacs!
Mr. President! Let the killing stop!
Word of honor, it's O.K. if the killing stops!

✳

Let the killing stop.

I now go over the head of every super patriot and ruler on Earth. I quote God Almighty, who said this: Thou shalt not kill.

4
HOW TO MAKE MONEY
AND FIND LOVE!

Fredonia College, Fredonia, New York,
May 20, 1978

As if that information weren't enough. Vonnegut explains
why we laugh at jokes, why we are lonely, and why there are
really six seasons in the year instead of only four.

Your class spokesperson has just said that she is
sick and tired of hearing people say, "I'm glad I'm
not a young person these days." All I can say is, "I'm
glad I'm not a young person these days."

Your college's president wished to exclude all
negative thinking from his farewell to you, and so
has asked me to make this announcement: "All per-
sons who still owe parking fees are to pay up before

53

leaving the property, or there will be monkey business with their transcripts."

When I was a boy in Indianapolis, there was a humorist there named Kin Hubbard. He wrote a few lines for *The Indianapolis News* every day. Indianapolis needs all the humorists it can get. He was often as witty as Oscar Wilde. He said, for instance, that prohibition was better than no liquor at all. He said that whoever named near-beer was a poor judge of distance.

I assume that the really important stuff has been spread out over your four years here and that you have no need of anything much from me. This is lucky for me. I have only this to say, basically: this is the end—this is childhood's end for certain. "Sorry about that," as they used to say in the Vietnam War.

Perhaps you have read the novel *Childhood's End* by Arthur C. Clarke, one of the few masterpieces in the field of science fiction. All of the others were written by me. In Clarke's novel, the characters undergo spectacular evolutionary change. The children become very different from the parents, less physical,

more spiritual—and one day they form up into a sort
of column of light which spirals out into the universe,
its mission unknown. The book ends there. You
seniors, however, look a great deal like your parents,
and I doubt that you will go radiantly into space as
soon as you have your diplomas in hand. It is far
more likely that you will go to Buffalo or Rochester
or East Quogue—or Cohoes.

And I suppose you will all want money and true
love, among other things. I will tell you how to
make money: work very hard. I will tell you how to
win love: wear nice clothing and smile all the time.
Learn the words to all the latest songs.

What other advice can I give you? Eat lots
of bran to provide necessary bulk in your diet.
The only advice my father ever gave me was this:
"Never stick anything in your ear." The tini-
est bones in your body are inside your ears, you
know—and your sense of balance, too. If you mess
around with your ears, you could not only become
deaf, but you could also start falling down all the
time. So just leave your ears completely alone.
They're fine, just the way they are.

Don't murder anybody—even though New York State does not use the death penalty.

That's about it.

One sort of optional thing you might do is to realize there are six seasons instead of four. The poetry of four seasons is all wrong for this part of the planet, and this may explain why we are so depressed so much of the time. I mean, Spring doesn't feel like Spring a lot of the time, and November is all wrong for Fall and so on. Here is the truth about the seasons: Spring is May and June! What could be springier than May and June? Summer is July and August. Really hot, right? Autumn is September and October. See the pumpkins? Smell those burning leaves. Next comes the season called "Locking." That is when Nature shuts everything down. November and December aren't Winter. They're Locking. Next comes Winter, January and February. Boy! Are they ever cold! What comes next? Not Spring. Unlocking comes next. What else could April be?

One more optional piece of advice: if you ever have to give a speech, start with a joke, if you know

one. For years I have been looking for the best joke in the world. I think I know what it is. I will tell it to you, but you have to help me. You have to say, "No," when I hold up my hand like this. All right? Don't let me down.

Do you know why cream is so much more expensive than milk?

AUDIENCE: No.

It is because the cows hate to squat on those little bottles.

That is the best joke I know. One time when I worked for the General Electric Company over in Schenectady, I had to write speeches for company officers. I put that joke about the cows and the little bottles in a speech for a vice president. He was reading along, and he had never heard the joke before. He couldn't stop laughing, and he had to be led away from the podium with a nosebleed. I was fired the next day.

How do jokes work? The beginning of each good one challenges you to think. We are such earnest animals. When I asked you about cream, you could not help yourselves. You really tried to think of

a sensible answer. Why does a chicken cross the
road? Why does a fireman wear red suspenders?
Why did they bury George Washington on the side
of a hill?

The second part of the joke announces that
nobody wants you to think, nobody wants to hear
your wonderful answer. You are so relieved to at
last meet somebody who doesn't demand that you
be intelligent. You laugh for joy.

I have in fact designed this entire speech so as to
allow you to be as stupid as you like, without strain,
and without penalties of any kind. I have even
written a ridiculous song for the occasion. It lacks
music, but we are up to our necks in composers.
One is sure to come along. The words go like this:

Adios to teachers and pneumonia.
If I find out where the party is,
I'll telephone ya.
I love you so much, Sonya,
That I am going to buy you a begonia.
You love me, too, doan ya, Sonya?

See—you were trying to guess what the next rhyme
was going to be. Nobody cares how smart you are.

I am being so silly because I pity you so much.
I pity all of us so much. Life is going to be very
tough again, just as soon as this is over. And the
most useful thought we can hold when all hell cuts
loose again is that we are not members of different
generations, as unlike, as some people would have
us believe, as Eskimos and Australian Aborigines.
We are all so close to each other in time that we
should think of ourselves as brothers and sisters.
I have several children—seven, to be exact—too
many children for an atheist, certainly. Whenever
my children complain about the planet to me, I
say, "Shut up! I just got here myself. Who do you
think I am—Methuselah? You think I like the
news of the day any better than you do? You're
wrong."

We are all experiencing more or less the same
lifetime now.

What is it the slightly older people want from the
slightly younger people? They want credit for having
survived so long, and often imaginatively, under dif-

ficult conditions. Slightly younger people are intoler-
ably stingy about giving them credit for that.

What is it the slightly younger people want from
the slightly older people? More than anything, I
think, they want acknowledgement, and without
further ado, that they are without question women
and men now. Slightly older people are intolerably
stingy about making any such acknowledgement.

Therefore, I take it upon myself to pronounce
those about to graduate women and men. No one
must ever treat them like children again. Neither
must they ever act like children—ever again.

This is what is known as a puberty ceremony.

I realize that it is coming a little late, but better
late than never. Every primitive society ever stud-
ied has had a puberty ceremony, at which former
children became unchallengeably women and men.
Some Jewish communities still honor this old prac-
tice, of course, and benefit from it, in my opinion.
But, by and large, ultramodern, massively industri-
alized societies like ours have decided to do without
puberty ceremonies—unless you want to count the
issuance of drivers' licenses at the age of 16. If you

want to count that as a puberty ceremony, then it
has a highly unusual feature: a judge can take your
puberty away again, even if you're as old as I am.

Another event in the lives of American and Euro-
pean males which might be considered a puberty
ceremony is war. If a male comes home from a war,
especially with serious wounds, everybody agrees:
here indeed is a man. When I came home to India-
napolis from the Second World War in Germany,
an uncle of mine said to me, "By golly—you look
like a man now." I wanted to strangle him. If I had,
he would have been the first German I'd killed. I
was a man before I went to war, but he was damned
if he would say so.

I suggest to you that the withholding of a puberty
ceremony from young males in our society is a scheme,
devised cunningly but subconsciously, to make those
males eager to go to war, no matter how terrible or
unjust a war may be. There are just wars, too, of course.
The war I was eager to go to happened to be a just one.

And when does a female stop being a little girl and
become a woman, with all the rights and privileges
appertaining thereto? We all know the answer in our

bones: when she has a baby in wedlock, of course. If she has that first baby out of wedlock, she is still a child. What could be simpler or more natural and more obvious than that—or, in these days and in this society, at least, more unjust, irrelevant, and just plain stupid?

I think we had better, for our own safety, reinstate puberty ceremonies.

I not only pronounce those about to graduate as women and men. With all the powers vested in me, I pronounce them Clarks as well. Most of you know, I'm sure, that all white people named Clark are descended from inhabitants of the British Isles who were remarkable for being able to read and write. A black person named Clark, of course, would be descended, most likely, from someone who was forced to work without pay or rights of any kind by a white person named Clark. An interesting family—the Clarks.

I realize that you graduates are all specialized in some way. But you have spent most of the past sixteen or more years learning to read and write. People who can do those things well, as you can, are miracles and, in my opinion, entitle us to suspect that we may be civilized after all. It is terri-

bly hard to learn to read and write. It takes simply forever. When we scold our schoolteachers about the low reading scores of their students, we pretend that it is the easiest thing in the world: to teach a person to read and write. Try it sometime, and you will discover that it is nearly impossible.

What good is being a Clark, now that we have computers and movies and television? Clarking, a wholly human enterprise, is sacred. Machinery is not. Clarking is the most profound and effective form of meditation practiced on this planet, and far surpasses any dream experienced by a Hindu on a mountaintop. Why? Because Clarks, by reading well, can think the thoughts of the wisest and most interesting human minds throughout all history. When Clarks meditate, even if they themselves have only mediocre intellects, they do it with the thoughts of angels. What could be more sacred than that?

So much for puberty and Clarking. Only two major subjects remain to be covered: loneliness and boredom. No matter what age any of us is now, we are going to be bored and lonely during what remains of our lives.

We are so lonely because we don't have enough friends and relatives. Human beings are supposed to live in stable, like-minded, extended families of fifty people or more.

Your class spokesperson mourned the collapse of the institution of marriage in this country. Marriage is collapsing because our families are too small. A man cannot be a whole society to a woman, and a woman cannot be a whole society to a man. We try, but it is scarcely surprising that so many of us go to pieces.

So I recommend that everybody here join all sorts of organizations, no matter how ridiculous, simply to get more people in his or her life. It does not matter much if all the other members are morons. Quantities of relatives of any sort are what we need.

As for boredom: Friedrich Wilhelm Nietzsche, a German philosopher who died seventy-eight years ago, had this to say: "Against boredom even the gods contend in vain." We are supposed to be bored. It is a part of life. Learn to put up with it, or you will not be what I have declared the members of this graduating class to be: mature women and men.

I come to a close now by noting that the press,

whose business is to know and understand every-
thing, often find young people to be apathetic
(especially when pundits and commentators can't
think of anything else to write about or talk about).
The new generation of graduates has failed to eat a
certain vitamin or mineral perhaps, iron perhaps.
They have tired blood. They need Geritol. Well, as
a member of a zippier generation, with sparkle in
its eyes and a snap in its stride, let me tell you what
kept us as high as kites a lot of the time: hatred.
All my life I've had people to hate—from Hitler to
Nixon, not that those two are at all comparable in
their villainy. It is a tragedy, perhaps, that human
beings can get so much energy and enthusiasm
from hate. If you want to feel ten feet tall and as
though you could run a hundred miles without
stopping, hate beats pure cocaine any day. Hitler
resurrected a beaten, bankrupt, half-starved nation
with hatred and nothing more. Imagine that.

So it seems quite likely to me that young people of
today in the United States of America are not in fact
apathetic, but only look that way to people who are
used to getting their ecstasies from hatred, among

other things, of course. The members of your gradu-
ating class are not sleepy, are not listless, are not apa-
thetic. They are simply performing the experiment
of doing without hate. Hate is the missing vitamin or
mineral or whatever in their diet, they have sensed
correctly that hate, in the long run, is about as nour-
ishing as cyanide. This is a very exciting thing they
are doing, and I wish them well.

5
ADVICE TO GRADUATING WOMEN (THAT ALL MEN SHOULD KNOW!)

Agnes Scott College, Decatur, Georgia,
May 15, 1999

In which the author answers the question that Freud asked,
but never could figure out: "What do women want?" For
good measure, he also reveals what men really want.

We love you, are proud of you, expect good things
from you, and wish you well.

This is a long-delayed puberty ceremony. You are
at last officially full-grown women—what you were
biologically by the age of 15 or so. I am as sorry
as I can be that it took so much time and money
before you could at last be licensed as grown-ups.

Kin Hubbard, a newspaper humorist in my

hometown of Indianapolis when I was growing up, wrote a joke a day for *The Indianapolis News.* One day, I remember, he said, "It's no disgrace to be poor, but it might as well be." He said this about graduation addresses: "I think it would be better if colleges spread out the really important stuff over four years, instead of saving it all up for the very end."

But that's what you're going to get from me: all the really important stuff at the very end.

I am so smart I know what is wrong with the world. Everybody asks during and after our wars, and the continuing terrorist attacks all over the globe, "What's gone wrong?"

What has gone wrong is that too many people, including high school kids and heads of state, are obeying the Code of Hammurabi, a King of Babylonia who lived nearly four thousand years ago. And you can find his code echoed in the Old Testament, too. Are you ready for this?

"An eye for an eye and a tooth for a tooth."

A categorical imperative for all who live in obedience to the Code of Hammurabi, which includes

heroes of every cowboy show and gangster show you ever saw, is this: Every injury, real or imagined, shall be avenged. Somebody's going to be really sorry.

(Horrible laugh.)

Bombs away—or whatever.

When Jesus Christ was nailed to a cross, he said, "Forgive them, Father, they know not what they do." What kind of a man was that? Any real man, obeying the Code of Hammurabi, would have said, "Kill them, Dad, and all their friends and relatives, and make their deaths slow and painful."

His greatest legacy to us, in my humble opinion, consists of only twelve words. They are the antidote to the poison of the Code of Hammurabi, a formula almost as compact as Albert Einstein's "$E = mc^2$."

Jesus of Nazareth told us to say these twelve words when we prayed: "Forgive us our trespasses as we forgive those who trespass against us."

Bye-bye, Code of Hammurabi.

And for those words alone, he deserves to be called "the Prince of Peace."

Every act of war, every act of violence, even by a

paranoid schizophrenic, celebrates Hammurabi and shows contempt for Jesus Christ.

Is anybody here a Presbyterian?

I want to warn you: Many people have been burned alive in public for believing what you believe. So watch your backs after you get out of here.

Some of you may know that I am a Humanist, or Freethinker, as were my parents and grand-parents and great grandparents—and so not a Christian. By being a Humanist, I am honoring my mother and father, which the Bible tells us is a good thing to do.

But I say with all my American ancestors, "If what Jesus said was good, and so much of it was absolutely beautiful, what does it matter if he was God or not?"

If Christ hadn't delivered the Sermon on the Mount, with its message of mercy and pity, I wouldn't want to be a human being.

I would just as soon be a rattlesnake.

Revenge provokes revenge which provokes revenge which provokes revenge—forming an unbroken chain of death and destruction linking

nations of today to barbarous tribes of thousands and thousands of years ago.

We may never dissuade leaders of our nation or any other nation from responding vengefully, violently, to every insult or injury. In this, the Age of Television, they will continue to find irresistible the temptation to become entertainers, to compete with movies by blowing up bridges and police stations and factories and so on.

Fires, explosions. Come look. Oh my gosh—hey wow.

To quote the late Irving Berlin: "There's no business like show business."

But in our personal lives, our inner lives, at least, we can learn to live without the sick excitement, without the kick of having scores to settle with this particular person, or that bunch of people, or that particular institution or race or nation.

And we can then reasonably ask forgiveness for our trespasses, since we forgive those who trespass against us. And we can teach our children and then our grandchildren to do the same—so that they, too, can never be a threat to anyone.

OK?

Amen.

Not that there hasn't been a lot of good news, along with the bad, long before you got here. I am talking about the birth of works of art. Music, paintings. Statues, buildings, poems, stories, plays, and essays, and movies (you bet), and humane ideas—which make us feel honored to be members of the human race.

What can you yourselves contribute? You've come this far anyway, and it wasn't easy. And I now recite a famous line by the poet Robert Browning, with one small change. I have replaced his word "man," which in his time was taken to mean "human being," with the word "woman."

May I say, too, that his wife Elizabeth Barrett was as great a poet as he was: "How do I love thee? Let me count the ways . . ." and so on.

While I'm at it, get a load of this: The atomic bomb which we dropped on the people of Hiroshima was first envisioned by a woman, not a man. She was, of course, Mary Wollstonecraft Shelley. She didn't call it an "atomic bomb." She called it "the monster of Frankenstein."

But back to Robert Browning, and what he said about anyone who hopes to make the world better. Again, I've changed his word "man" to "woman" for this occasion:

"A woman's reach should exceed her grasp, or what's a heaven for?"

And of course the original: "A man's reach should exceed his grasp, or what's a heaven for?"

Sigmund Freud said he didn't know what women wanted. I am so smart I not only know what is wrong with the world, the Code of Hammurabi, but I know what women want. Women want a whole lot of people to talk to. What do they want to talk about? They want to talk about everything.

Men want a lot of pals—and they don't want people to get mad at them.

Some of you may become psychologists or ministers. In either case, you are going to have to deal with men, women, and children whose lives are being damaged by our country's astronomical divorce rate. You should know that when a husband and wife fight, it may seem to be about money or sex or power.

But what they're really yelling at each other

about is loneliness. What they're really saying is, "You're not enough people."

Back when most human beings lived in extended families and lived in the same part of the world for the whole of their lives, a marriage was really something to celebrate. Wedding guests laughed instead of cried. The groom was going to get a lot of new pals, and the bride was going to get a whole new bunch of people to talk to about everything.

Nowadays, most of us when we marry get just one person—and, oh sure, maybe a few scruffy in-laws, ready to kill each other, and living hundreds of miles away, if you're lucky—in someplace like Vancouver, British Columbia, or Hollywood, Florida.

So again: If any of you educated people find yourselves in a therapeutic situation vis-à-vis a marriage on the rocks, please realize that the real problem may not be money or sex or power or how to raise a kid. The real trouble with the wife, as far as the husband is concerned, may be that she isn't enough people. The real trouble with the husband, as far as the wife is concerned, may be that he isn't enough people.

If you determine that that really is what they've been yelling at each other about, tell them to become more people for each other by joining a synthetic extended family—like the Hell's Angels, perhaps, or the American Humanist Association, with headquarters in Amherst, New York—or the nearest church.

I met a man in Nigeria one time, an Ibo who had six hundred relatives he knew quite well. His wife had just had a baby, the best possible news in any extended family.

They were going to take it to meet all its relatives, Ibos of all ages and sizes and shapes. It would even meet other babies, cousins not much older than it was. Everybody who was big enough and steady enough was going to get to hold it, cuddle it, gurgle to it, and say how pretty it was, or handsome.

Wouldn't you have loved to be that baby?

Here is a fact: this wonderful speech is already more than twice as long as the most efficient, effective oration in American history, Abraham Lincoln's address on the battlefield at Gettysburg.

As I speak, the very air we breathe is vibrant with

words and images from CNN. In the early days
of radio, I remember, people living too close to the
transmitter of KDKA in Pittsburgh used to receive
soap operas in their bedsprings and bridgework.

And nowadays, surely, TV is such a pervasive
part of so many Americans' lives that they might
as well be hearing Wolf Blitzer in their bedsprings
and bridgework. And I have a son-in-law who has
been swallowed by his computer. He disappeared
into it, and I'm not sure we can ever get him back
out again. And he has a wife and kids!

There was a time when a graduation speaker,
looking out at a sea of beauty and innocence such
as this one, would warn you about all the sewer
rats you will meet as you flow out of here and into
the gutters of the real world. I mean lascivious,
untruthful men, tinhorn Casanovas and sociopathic
Lochinvars. But *Cosmopolitan* and *Elle* magazines
have told you all about them—and told you how to
protect yourselves.

If somebody says he loves you, check it out.

And your State and Federal Governments, thank
goodness, have told you not to smoke cigarettes,

which are evil incarnate. . . . Who in his or her right
mind doesn't hate evil with a passion?

Cigarettes are very bad for you—but cigars are
very good for you. Cigars are so healthful that there
is a magazine devoted to them, with pictures of
cigar-smoking celebrities on the cover.

Cigars, of course, are made of trail mix—of nuts
and raisins and granola. Why don't you all eat a
cigar at bedtime tonight?

No cholesterol.

Firearms are also good for you. No fat, no nico-
tine, and no cholesterol.

Ask your Congressperson if this isn't true.

And God bless the State and Federal Govern-
ments for taking such good care of the public health.

I hope you know that television and computers are
no more your friends, and no more increasers of your
brainpower, than slot machines. All they want is for
you to sit still and buy all kinds of junk, and play the
stock market as though it were a game of blackjack.

And only well-informed, warm-hearted people
can teach others things they'll always remember
and love. Computers and TV don't do that.

A computer teaches a child what a computer can become.

An educated human being teaches a child what a child can become.

Bad men just want your bodies. TVs and computers want your money, which is even more disgusting. It's so much more dehumanizing!

Given a choice, wouldn't you rather have somebody like your body more than your money?

Forbes magazine asked me recently what my favorite technologies were, and I said a corner mailbox, my address book, and the *Encyclopedia Britannica*. The *Britannica* is arranged alphabetically, so you can find out all kinds of stuff, if you know your ABCs.

And putting a letter in a corner mailbox is like feeding a great big bullfrog painted blue.

I thank you for becoming educated. By becoming reasonable and informed persons, you have made this a more rational world than it was before you got here. I give you my word of honor that you graduates are near the very top of the best news I ever heard. By working so hard at becoming wise

and reasonable and well-informed, you have made
our little planet, our precious little moist, blue-green
ball, a saner place than it was before you got here.

Thanks, and God bless those who made it pos-
sible for you to improve your minds and souls in the
company of students from every part of this coun-
try, and foreign nations besides.

What fun, eh? I should say.

Most of you are preparing to enter fields unat-
tractive to greedy persons, such as education and
the healing arts. Teaching, may I say, is the noblest
profession of all in a democracy.

Some of you will become mothers. I don't recom-
mend it, but these things happen.

If that should fall to your lot, you may find compen-
sation in these words by the poet William Ross Wal-
lace: "The hand that rocks the cradle rules the world."

And keep that kid the hell away from computers
and TV sets, unless you want it to be a lonesome
imbecile, who steals money from your purse so it
can buy stuff.

Don't give up on books. They feel so good—their
friendly heft. The sweet reluctance of their pages

when you turn them with your sensitive fingertips.
A large part of our brains is devoted to deciding
whether what our hands are touching is good or bad
for us. Any brain worth a nickel knows books are
good for us.

And don't try to make yourself an extended fam-
ily out of ghosts on the Internet.

Get yourself a Harley and join the Hell's Angels
instead.

Every graduation pep talk I've ever given has
ended with words about my father's kid brother,
Alex Vonnegut, a Harvard educated insurance
agent in Indianapolis, who was well-read and wise.

The first graduation at which I spoke, inciden-
tally, was at what was then a women's college—
Bennington, in Vermont. The Vietnam War was
going on, and the graduates wore no make-up, to
show how ashamed and sad they were.

But about my Uncle Alex, who is up in Heaven
now. One of the things he found objectionable about
human beings was that they so rarely noticed it when
they were happy. He himself did his best to acknowl-
edge it when times were sweet. We could be drink-

ing lemonade in the shade of an apple tree in the summertime, and Uncle Alex would interrupt the conversation to say, "If this isn't nice, what is?"

So I hope that you will do the same for the rest of your lives. When things are going sweetly and peacefully, please pause a moment, and then say out loud, "If this isn't nice, what is?"

Let that be the motto of your class: "If this isn't nice, what is?"

That's one favor I've asked of you. Now I ask for another one. I ask it not only of the graduates, but of everyone here, parents and teachers as well. I'll want a show of hands after I ask this question.

How many of you have had a teacher at any level of your education who made you more excited to be alive, prouder to be alive, than you had previously believed possible?

Hold up your hands, please.

Now take down your hands and say the name of that teacher to someone else and tell them what that teacher did for you.

All done?

If this isn't nice, what is?

6
HOW TO HAVE SOMETHING
MOST BILLIONAIRES DON'T

Rice University, Houston, Texas,
October 12, 2001

And learn to love your destiny!

Hello.

I have not calculated how much your diplomas cost in time and money. Whatever those ballpark figures are, they surely deserve this reaction from me today: Wow. Wow. Wow.

Thank you, and God bless you and those who made it possible for you to study at an American university. By becoming informed and reasonable and capable adults, you have made this a better world than it was before you got here.

Have we met before? No. But I have thought a lot about people like you. You men here are Adam. You women are Eve. Who hasn't thought a lot about Adam and Eve?

This is Eden, and you're about to be kicked out. Why? You ate the knowledge apple. It's in your tummies now.

And who am I? I used to be Adam. But now I am Methuselah.

So what does this Methuselah have to say to you, since he has lived so long? I'll pass on to you what another Methuselah said to me. He's Joe Heller, author, as you know, of *Catch-22*. We were at a party thrown by a multi-billionaire out on Long Island, and I said, "Joe, how does it make you feel to realize that only yesterday our host probably made more money than *Catch-22*, one of the most popular books of all time, has grossed worldwide over the past forty years?"

Joe said to me, "I have something he can never have."

I said, "What's that, Joe?"

And he said, "The knowledge that I've got enough."

His example may be of comfort to many of you Adams and Eves, who in later years will have to admit that something has gone terribly wrong—and that, despite the education you received here, you have somehow failed to become billionaires.

Well-dressed people ask me sometimes, with their teeth bared, as though they were about to bite me, if I believe in a redistribution of wealth. I can only reply that it doesn't matter what I think, that wealth is already being redistributed every hour, often in ways that are absolutely fantastic.

Nobel Prizes are peanuts when compared with what a linebacker for the Cowboys makes in a single season nowadays.

For about a hundred years now, the most lucrative prize for a person who made a really meaningful contribution to the culture of the world as a physicist, a chemist, a physiologist, a physician, a writer, or, God bless him or her, a maker of peace, has been the Nobel Prize. It is about a million dollars now. Those dollars come, incidentally, from a fortune made by a Swede who mixed clay with nitroglycerine and gave us dynamite.

KABOOM!

Alfred Nobel intended that his prizes make the
planet's most valuable inhabitants independently
wealthy, so that their work could not be inhibited or
bent this way or that way by powerful politicians or
wealthy patrons.

But one million dollars is only a white chip
now—in the worlds of sports and entertainment, on
Wall Street, in many lawsuits, as compensation for
executives of our larger corporations.

One million dollars in the tabloids and on the
evening news is "chump change" now.

I am reminded of a scene in a W. C. Fields movie,
in which he is watching a poker game in a saloon in
a gold-rush town. Fields announces his presence by
putting a one-hundred-dollar bill on the table. The
players barely look up from the game. One of them
finally says, "Give him a white chip."

But the cost of a college education, a minor frac-
tion of a million dollars, is anything but chump
change to most Americans. Have academic degrees
been a way to become famous and rich in the past?

In a few cases. You can no doubt name a handful

of celebrities who came from here. But most gradu-
ates, any place you care to name, have been of use
locally rather than nationally, and have commonly
been rewarded with modest amounts of money or
fame—or sometimes, more's the pity, with utterly
undeserved ingratitude.

In time, this will prove to have been the destiny
of most, but not all of you. You will find yourselves
building or strengthening your communities. Please
love that destiny, if it turns out to be yours—for com-
munities are all that's substantial about the world.

All the rest is hoop-la.

And for your footloose generation, that commu-
nity could as easily be New York City or Washing-
ton, DC, or Paris, or Houston—or Adelaide, Aus-
tralia, or Shanghai, or Kuala Lumpur.

Mark Twain, at the end of a profoundly mean-
ingful life, for which he never received a Nobel
Prize, asked himself what it was we all lived for. He
came up with six words which satisfied him. They
satisfy me, too. They should satisfy you:

"The good opinion of our neighbors."

Neighbors are people who know you, can see

you, can talk to you—to whom you may have been of some help or beneficial stimulation. They are not nearly as numerous as the fans, say, of Madonna or Michael Jordan.

To earn their good opinions, you should apply the special skills you have learned in college, and meet the standards of decency and honor and fair play set by exemplary books and elders.

It's even money that one of you will get a Nobel Prize. Wanna bet? It's only a million bucks, but what the heck. That's better than a sharp stick in the eye, as they say.

7
HOW MUSIC CURES OUR ILLS
(AND THERE ARE LOTS OF THEM)

Eastern Washington University, Spokane, Washington,
April 17, 2004

Vonnegut looks on the dark side, and finds that music,
waltzing, the blues, humor, and "people who behave
compassionately" make life worthwhile.

I was so innocent once that I still considered it possible that we could become the humane and reasonable America so many members of my generation used to dream of. We dreamed of such an America during the Great Depression, when there were no jobs. And then we fought and often died for that dream during the Second World War, when there was no peace.

91

But I know now that there is not a chance in hell of America's becoming humane and reasonable. That is because power corrupts us, and absolute power corrupts us absolutely. Human beings are chimpanzees who get crazy drunk on power. I myself have experienced that intoxication. I was once a Corporal.

By saying our leaders are power-drunk chimpanzees, am I in danger of wrecking the morale of our men and women fighting and dying in the Middle East? Their morale, like so many of their bodies, is already shot to pieces. They are being treated, as I never was, like toys a rich kid got for Christmas.

But I will say this:

No matter how corrupt and greedy our government and our corporations and our media and Wall Street and our religious and charitable organizations may become, the music will still be perfectly wonderful.

If I should ever die, God forbid, let this be my epitaph:

THE ONLY PROOF HE NEEDED OF THE EXISTENCE OF GOD WAS MUSIC.

And I have arranged for a Strauss waltz to be

played as you depart, so you can waltz the heck out of here when it is time to go. For those of you who don't know how to waltz, nothing could be easier and more human. You go step, slide, rest, step, slide, rest, step, slide, rest. Oom, pah, pah, oom, pah, pah.

Bill Gates doesn't seem to realize that we are dancing animals.

During our catastrophically idiotic war in Vietnam, the music just kept getting better and better. We lost that war, by the way. Order couldn't be restored in Indochina until the locals could finally kick us the hell out of there.

That war only made billionaires out of millionaires. This war[1] is making trillionaires out of billionaires. I call that progress.

And how come the people in countries we invade can't fight like ladies and gentlemen, in uniforms, and with tanks and helicopter gunships?

About music: I like Strauss and Mozart and all that, but I would be remiss not to mention the absolutely priceless gift which African Americans gave

1 The first Iraq War.

to the whole wide world when they were still in slavery. I mean the blues. All pop music today, jazz, swing, bebop, Elvis Presley, the Beatles, the Stones, rock 'n' roll, hip-hop, and on and on is derived from the blues.

How do I know it's a gift to the world? One of the best rhythm-and-blues combos I ever heard was three guys and a girl from Finland, playing in a club in Krakow, Poland.

The wonderful writer Albert Murray, who is a jazz historian among other things, told me that, during the era of slavery in this country, an atrocity from which we can never fully recover, the suicide rate per capita among slave owners was much higher than the suicide rate among slaves. Al Murray says he thinks this was because slaves had a way of dealing with depression, which their white owners did not. They could play the blues.

He says something else which also sounds right to me. He says the blues can't drive depression clear out of a house, but they can drive it into the corners of any room where they are being played.

I am, incidentally, honorary president of the American Humanist Association, having succeeded the late, great science-fiction writer Isaac Asimov in that utterly functionless capacity. We Humanists behave as honorably as we can without any expectations of rewards or punishments in an afterlife. We serve as best we can the only abstraction with which we have any real familiarity, which is our community.

We had a memorial service for Asimov a while back, and at one point I said, "Isaac is up in Heaven now." That was the funniest thing I could have said to an audience of Humanists. I rolled them in the aisles. It was several minutes before order could be restored.

If I should ever die, again God forbid, I hope some of you will say, "Kurt's up in Heaven now." That's my favorite joke.

How do Humanists feel about Jesus? If what he said was superb, how can it matter whether he was God or not?

When you get to my age, if you get to my age, and if you have reproduced, you will find yourself

asking your own children, who are themselves middle-aged, what life is all about. I have seven kids, four of them adopted.

Most of you here are the same age as my grandchildren. They, like you, are being royally shafted and lied to by our baby boomer corporations and government.

I put my big question about life to my biological son Mark. Mark is a pediatrician, and author of a memoir entitled *The Eden Express*. It is about his crackup, straitjacket and padded cell stuff, from which he recovered sufficiently to graduate from Harvard Medical School.

Dr. Vonnegut said this to his doddering old dad: "Father, we are here to help each other get through this thing, whatever it is." So I pass that on to you. Write it down, and put it in your computer, so you can forget it.

I have to say that's a pretty good sound bite, almost as good as, "Do unto others as you would have them do unto you." A lot of people think Jesus said that, because it is so much the sort of thing Jesus liked to say. But it was actually said by

Confucius, a Chinese, five hundred years before
there was that greatest and most humane of human
beings, named Jesus Christ.

The Chinese also gave us, via Marco Polo, pasta
and the formula for gunpowder. The Chinese were
so dumb they only used gunpowder for fireworks.

And everybody was so dumb back then that
nobody in either hemisphere even knew that there
was another one.

We've sure come a long way since then, only
seven hundred years ago. Sometimes I wish we
hadn't. I hate H-bombs and *The Jerry Springer Show*.

I love science. All Humanists do. I'm particularly
fond of the big bang theory. It goes like this: There
was once all this nothing, and it was so much noth-
ing that there wasn't even such a thing as nothing.
And then all of a sudden there was this great big
BANG, and that's where all this crap came from.
Forget the Bible.

Any questions?

You know what they should put over the entrance
to the Physics Department? Just that one word:
BANG!

You know what else I think? I think life is no
way to treat an animal, and not just people, but pigs
and chickens, too. Life just hurts too much.

Doesn't anything socialistic make you want to throw
up? Like great public schools or health insurance for all?

How about Jesus's Sermon on the Mount, the
Beatitudes?

Blessed are the meek,
for they shall inherit the earth.
Blessed are the merciful,
for they shall obtain mercy.
Blessed are the peacemakers,
for they shall be called the children of God, and so on.

Not exactly planks in a Republican platform.

For some reason, the most vocal Christians
among us never mention the Beatitudes. But, often
with tears in their eyes, they demand that the Ten
Commandments be posted in public buildings.
And of course that's Moses, not Jesus. I haven't
heard one of them demand that the Sermon on the
Mount, the Beatitudes, be posted anywhere.

"Blessed are the merciful" in a courtroom? "Blessed are the peacemakers" in the Pentagon? Give me a break!

Only kidding, but seriously: there is a tragic flaw in our precious Constitution, and I don't know what can be done to fix it. This is it: only nutcases want to be president.

This was true even in my high school. Only seriously disturbed people ran for class president.

We might have psychiatrists examine all the candidates. But who but a nutcase would want to be a psychiatrist?

But, when you stop to think about it, only a nutcase would want to be a human being, if he or she had a choice. Such treacherous, untrustworthy, lying, and greedy animals we are!

I wouldn't trust any one of you, no matter how friendly and innocent you may appear, any farther than I could throw you. Because you're human.

And for the love of God, as the Christians say, please don't trust me. I couldn't stand it.

My favorite song? It's "How Could You Believe Me When I Said I Loved You, When You Know I've Been a Liar All My Life?"

You want to know what I pray every night?

I go down on my old knees, next to my cot in the coal bin, and I pray with all my heart, "To Whom It May Concern: Couldn't you please put my soul inside a sea otter or a barn owl instead?" I would rather be a sea otter than a human being, even if there were another oil spill.

You want to know what the British mathematician and philosopher Bertrand Russell called this planet? He said it was "the Lunatic Asylum of the Universe." And he said the inmates had taken over, and we were tormenting each other and trashing the joint. And he wasn't talking about the germs or the elephants. He meant we the people.

Lord Russell lived to be almost a hundred. His dates are 1872 to 1970 AD. What does "AD" signify? That commemorates an asylum inmate who was nailed to a wooden cross by a bunch of other inmates. With him still conscious, they—no kidding—hammered spikes through his wrists and insteps, and into the wood. Then they set the cross upright, so he had to dangle up there where

even the shortest person in the crowd could see him writhing this way and that.

Can you imagine people doing such a thing to a person?

No problem. That's entertainment. Ask the devout Roman Catholic Mel Gibson, who, as an act of piety, made a fortune with a movie about how Jesus was tortured. Never mind what Jesus said.

During the reign of King Henry the Eighth, founder of the Church of England, he had a counterfeiter boiled alive in public. Show biz again.

Mel Gibson's next movie should be *The Counterfeiter*. Box office records will again be broken.

One of the few good things about modern times: If you die horribly on television, you will not have died in vain. You will have entertained us.

And what did the great British historian Edward Gibbon have to say about the human record so far? He said, "History is indeed little more than the register of the crimes, follies and misfortunes of mankind."

The same can be said about this morning's issue of *The New York Times*.

Edward Gibbon's dates? 1737 to 1794 AD.

The French Algerian writer Albert Camus, who won a Nobel Prize for Literature in 1957, wrote that "there is but one truly serious philosophical problem, and that is suicide."

So there's another barrel of laughs from literature. Camus himself died in an automobile accident. His dates? 1913 to 1960 AD.

Listen: All great literature is about what a bummer it is to be a human being: *Moby-Dick, Huckleberry Finn, The Red Badge of Courage, The Iliad* and *The Odyssey, Crime and Punishment,* the Bible, and *The Charge of the Light Brigade.*

But I have to say this in defense of humankind: No matter in what era in history, including the Garden of Eden, everybody just got there. And, except for the Garden of Eden, there were already all these crazy games going on, which could make you act crazy, even if you weren't crazy to begin with. Some of the games which were already going on when you got here were love and hate, Liberalism and Conservatism, automobiles and credit cards and girls' basketball.

On the subject of crazy games already going on before any of us ever got here:

If you keep up with current events in the supermarket tabloids, you know that a team of Martian anthropologists has been studying our culture for the past ten years, since our culture is the only one worth a nickel on the whole damn planet. You can forget Brazil and Argentina.

Anyway: They went back home last week, because they knew how terrible global warming was about to be. Their space vehicle wasn't a flying saucer. It was more like a flying soup tureen. And they're little all right, only six inches high. But they aren't green. They're mauve.

And their little mauve leader, by way of farewell, said in that teeny-weeny, tanny-wanny, toney-woney little voice of hers that there were two things about American culture no Martian would ever understand.

"What is it," she squeaked, "what can it possibly be about blow jobs and golf?"

Even crazier than golf, though, is modern American politics, where, thanks to TV, and for the con-

venience of TV, you can be only one of two kinds of human beings, either a Liberal or a Conservative.

Actually, this same sort of thing happened to the people of England ten generations ago, and Sir William Gilbert, of the radical team of Gilbert and Sullivan, wrote these words for a song about it back then:

> I often think it's comical
> How nature always does contrive
> That every boy and every gal,
> That's born into the world alive,
> Is either a little Liberal,
> Or a little Conservative.

Which one are you in this country, and it's practically a law of life that you have to be one or the other? If you aren't one or the other, you might as well be a doughnut.

If some of you still haven't decided, I'll make it easy for you.

If you want to take my guns away from me, and you're all for murdering fetuses, and love it when homosexuals marry each other, and want to give

them kitchen showers, and you're for the poor, you're a Liberal.

If you are against those perversions and for the rich, you're a Conservative.

What could be simpler?

A show of hands, please: How many of you are Liberals?

On the subject of homosexuality: If you really want to hurt your parents, and you don't have the nerve to be gay, the least you can do is go into the arts. And in a few minutes I'll give a lesson in creative writing.

In the meanwhile, though, I want to talk about our government's war on drugs. It's certainly a lot better than no drugs at all. It was illegal mescaline which put my son Mark into a loony bin for a little while.

But get this: The two most widely abused and addictive and destructive of all substances are both perfectly legal. One, of course is ethyl alcohol. And President George W. Bush, no less, and by his own admission, was smashed or tiddley-poo or four sheets to the wind a good deal of the time from when he was 16 until he was 41. When he was

41, he says, Jesus appeared to him, and made him knock off the sauce, stop gargling nose paint.

Other drunks have seen pink elephants.

And what the heck, he didn't make any of the big decisions, and couldn't, and wouldn't want to in any case.

All he had to do was say he would not cut and run, no matter what happened in Iraq or Afghanistan. Where in heck can you cut and run to from Crawford, Texas? Dubuque, Iowa? Spokane?

And you know why I think he was so pissed off at Arabs? They invented algebra.

Arabs also invented the numbers we use, including a symbol for nothing, which nobody else had ever had before.

You think Arabs are dumb? Try doing long division with Roman numerals.

We're spreading democracy, are we? Same way European explorers brought Christianity to the Indians, who we now call "Native Americans." There's this story about Spaniards who were about to burn a Native American alive because he had been uppity some way. And he was lashed

to the stake, about to entertain, and a Spaniard
tied a cross to the end of a long stick, and he held
it up so the Native American could kiss it.

And the Native American asked why he should
kiss it, and the Spaniard said if he kissed it he could
get into Heaven. And the Native American asked if
there were Spaniards in Heaven. He was told there
were, and the Native American said he certainly
didn't want to go there.

How ungrateful he was! How ungrateful are the
people of Baghdad.

So let's give another big tax cut to the super-rich.
That'll teach Al Qaeda a lesson it won't soon forget.
Hail to the Chief.

That chief and his cohorts had as little to do
with democracy as those Spaniards had to do
with Jesus. We the people had absolutely no say
in whatever they chose to do next. In case you
hadn't noticed, they cleaned out the treasury,
passing it out to pals in the war and national
security rackets, leaving your generation and the
next one with a perfectly enormous debt which
you'll be asked to repay.

Nobody let out a peep when they did that to you, because big money and TV have disconnected every burglar alarm in the Constitution: the House, the Senate, the Supreme Court and the FBI, and We the People.

About my own history of foreign substance abuse. By the grace of God or whatever, I am not an alcoholic, largely a matter of genes. I take a couple of drinks now and then, and will do it again tonight. But two is my limit. No problem.

I am of course notoriously hooked on cigarettes. I keep hoping the things will kill me. A fire at one end and a fool at the other.

And I've been a coward about heroin and cocaine and LSD and so on, afraid they might put me over the edge, and, unlike my son Mark, I might never come back again. I did smoke a joint of marijuana one time with Jerry Garcia of the Grateful Dead, just to be sociable. It didn't seem to do anything to me, one way or the other, so I never did it again.

But I'll tell you one thing: I once had a high that not even crack cocaine could match. That was when

I got my first driver's license! Look out, world, here comes Kurt Vonnegut. I'm what a car is now. I'm a hundred horsepower now, which is eleven hundred manpower, so don't mess with me. Hiya, Babe, you want a lift somewhere?

And my car back then, a Studebaker, as I recall, was powered, as are almost all means of transportation and other machinery today, and electric power plants and furnaces, by the most addictive and destructive drugs of all, which are fossil fuels, so easy to set afire.

When you got here, even when I got here, the industrialized world was already hopelessly hooked on fossil fuels, and very soon now there won't be any more of those. Cold turkey.

You've heard of "crack babies"? Those are babies who come into the world already hooked on crack because their mothers were hooked on crack. Well, we are all fossil fuel babies.

As I speak, we are burning the last whiffs and drops and chunks of fossil fuels in a binge of thermodynamic whoopee. And while we do that, our waste products continue to make the air unbreath-

able and the water undrinkable, and more and more life forms are dying because of us.

This is a university, isn't it? Isn't it OK to tell young people the truth here? I mean this isn't like TV news, is it?

And here's what I think the truth is: we are all addicts of fossil fuels in a state of denial, about to face cold turkey.

And like so many addicts about to face cold turkey, we are now committing violent crimes to get what little is left of what we're hooked on.

But relax. I've got a joke that will dispel the gloom. It's another Martian joke. This is it, and no matter what, we've still got music and our sense of humor:

There's bad news and good news tonight, my friends. The bad news is the Martians have landed in New York City and are staying at the Waldorf-Astoria.

The good news is they only eat homeless people and they pee gasoline.

Put some of that pee in a Ferrari, and you can go a hundred miles an hour. If you're a guy, you can have

babes like you can't believe. Put some in an airplane
and you can go as fast as a bullet, and drop all kinds
of crap on the Arabs below. Put some in a school bus,
it'll get the kids to and from school. Put some in a fire
engine, and it will get firemen to a fire, so they can
put the fire out. Put some in a Honda, and it'll get
you to work, and then back home again.

And wait till you hear what the Martians
poop. It's uranium. Just one of them can light
and heat every home and school and church and
business in Tacoma.

What's it like to be my age? I can't parallel park
worth a darn anymore, so please don't watch while
I try to do it. And gravity has become a lot less
friendly and manageable than it used to be.

I have also become a flaming neuter. I am
as celibate as fifty percent of the heterosexual
Roman Catholic clergy. And celibacy is no root
canal. It's so cheap and convenient. You don't
have to do or say anything afterward, because
there is no afterward.

And when my tantrum, which is what I call my
TV set, flashes boobs and smiles in my face, and

says everybody but me is going to get laid tonight, and this is a national emergency, so I've got to rush out and buy a car or pills, or a folding gymnasium I can hide under my bed, I laugh like a hyena. I know and you know that millions and millions of good Americans, present company not excepted, are not going to get laid tonight.

And we flaming neuters vote! So I am looking forward to the day when the President of the United States, no less, who probably isn't going to get laid that night, declares a National Neuter Pride Day. And out of our closets we'll come by the millions. Shoulders squared, chins held high, we'll go marching up Main Streets all over this boob-crazed democracy of ours, and laughing like hyenas.

But hey, listen: I got a letter from a sappy woman a while back. She knew I was sappy, too, a Franklin Roosevelt Democrat, a friend of the working stiffs. She was about to have a baby, not mine. She wanted to know if it was a mistake to bring an innocent little baby into a world as awful as this one is. I told her that what made life

almost worth living for me was the saints I met.
These were people who behaved compassionately
and capably, no matter what, and they could
be anywhere.

So maybe some of you tonight are or may become
saints for her child to meet. Most of us are loaded
with Original Sin. But a surprising number of us,
not me, God knows, are loaded with Original Vir-
tue. Ain't that sweet?

So now it's time for me to teach creative writing.

First rule: Do not use semicolons. They are trans-
vestite hermaphrodites, representing nothing. All
they do is show you've been to college.

And I realize that some of you may be having
trouble deciding whether I am kidding or not. So
from now on I will thumb my nose at you when
I'm kidding.

For instance? Join the National Guard or the
Marines and teach democracy. (NOSE)

If I give you the finger, (FINGER) it means
Spokane is about to be attacked by Al Qaeda. In
that case wave flags, if you have them. That always
seems to scare them away. Please don't get the two

signals mixed up, or you might accidentally start World War III.

I will now exit while *The Blue Danube* comes over the PA system. Please waltz out as you leave.

8
WHAT THE "GHOST DANCE" OF THE NATIVE AMERICANS AND THE FRENCH PAINTERS WHO LED THE CUBIST MOVEMENT HAVE IN COMMON

The University of Chicago, Chicago, Illinois,
February 17, 1994

In which Vonnegut tells how his own fiction writing
was inspired by the professor who was "low man on the
totem pole" in the University of Chicago Anthropology
Department.

A young woman told me a couple of years ago that
she had applied for admission here. The man who
interviewed her asked her why she had found the
place attractive. She said it was because Philip
Roth and I had both gone here, along with many

other considerations, of course. He replied that Philip and I were precisely the sorts of persons who never should have gone here. What could he have meant by that? If he is in this audience, I would appreciate meeting and talking to him afterward.

I came here in 1946, immediately following my participation in a war. It was the Second World War, a name and event worthy of H. G. Wells. That war ended with our dropping atomic bombs on the civilians, and their pets and house plants, of Hiroshima and Nagasaki, quite a surprise to one and all. That such bombs were possible was first demonstrated in the abandoned football stadium of this very university, where the importance of contact sports had been discounted. The university president at that time, Robert Maynard Hutchins, was famous for saying that, whenever he felt in need of exercise, he lay down until the feeling passed. He finally wound up in a California think tank.

So far as I know, the only Second World War weapon worth a nickel to come out of Harvard, which thinks it's such hot stuff, was Napalm or jellied gasoline.

I came here from Indianapolis. In those days, that was like a provincial Frenchman's coming to Paris, or an Austrian bumpkin's coming to Vienna, or, as in the case of Adolf Hitler, to Munich, Germany.

In those days, thanks again to Robert Maynard Hutchins, the undergraduate course consisted of only two years devoted to a study of the so-called Great Books. Philip Roth is a product of that short course. We would not meet until many years afterward. The graduate school was everything past what would have been the sophomore year at other American institutions. Like many returning veterans with more than two years' worth of credits from someplace else, I was admitted to this unconventional graduate school, with three or four years to go before qualifying for an MA.

The credits I brought with me were near-flunks in chemistry, physics, math, and biology. I had actually twice flunked a course whose purpose is to exclude people like me from careers as scientists, which is thermodynamics.

Despite my inability to o'er-leap the intellec-

tual barrier of thermodynamics, or pile of shit, if you like, I still wanted to be respected as a person who thought scientifically, who loved the truth, the whole truth, and nothing but the truth. It was obvious that only a pseudoscience was a possibility for me. Ideally, I thought, it should be a pseudoscience socially superior to astrology, meteorology, hairdressing, economics, or embalming.

The two most prominent such, then as now, were psychoanalysis and cultural anthropology. Both were based, then as now, on what had regularly sent innocent persons to the electric chair or the hot squat, which is human testimony, which is blah-blah-blah. I chose cultural anthropology. The result now stands before you.

Much has been written about the effects on institutions of higher learning of the sudden influx of veterans after my war. One thing it did was bamboozle many teachers whose authority and glamour was based on their having seen a lot more of life and the world than their students had. In seminars I would occasionally try to talk about something I had

observed about human beings while a soldier, as a prisoner of war, as a family man. I had a wife and kid then. This turned out to be very bad manners, like coming to a crap game with loaded dice. No fair.

Also: we were so innocent.

In retrospect, my trying to become a member of the anthropology department was like visiting a kibbutz, a kibbutz as described by Bruno Bettelheim in *The Children of the Dream*. We returning veterans were mildly interesting strangers to be treated politely, with our understanding and theirs that we would soon go away again. And we did.

At about that time there appeared in the *New Yorker* a series of stories by Ludwig Bemelmans about a busboy who assisted a waiter in a grand hotel in Paris. The waiter was named Mespoulets, "my little chickens." Mespoulets's specialty was serving persons the management didn't want to come back again.

Every academic department has a sort of Mespoulets, I think. We certainly had one in the Writers Workshop at the University of Iowa when

I taught there. The Mespoulets in the anthropology department in my time I will call Dr. Z, who is no longer among the living.

Dr. Z was lacking in the charm and stage presence fundamental to the reputation of a great cultural anthropologist. He was also having trouble getting published. So he was made thesis advisor for those of us the department's stars did not care to work with. He also gave a course in the summertime, when the rest of the department was on vacation or on a dig or whatever. The course could be about anything, since its real purpose was to entitle returning veterans to continue to receive living allowances from a grateful government. In order to make ends meet, I was working as a police reporter for the Chicago City News Bureau, practicing what might nowadays be called "urban anthropology."

Becoming one of Dr. Z's little chickens was one of the most fortunate things that ever happened to me, second only, perhaps, to my having been in Dresden when it was firebombed. He died a long time ago now, but many of his ideas live on with me. He died several years after I left. He was a

suicide. He had great big ideas about science, about art, about religion, about evolution, and on and on, which he expressed in his cockamamie summer course. Many of these, and surely the grandeur of his dealing with the biggest issues imaginable, are elements in my works of fiction.

I don't know if he left a suicide note. My guess is that he found it impossible to put his great big ideas on paper.

He had so many great big ideas that he gave me one for my thesis. I was a candidate for a master's degree, mind you, for the rank of Corporal in Academia. He said my dissertation should deal with the sort of leadership required if a radical change in a culture was to be effected. Why mess around?

So I did it. He told me to compare the leadership which inspired a peaceful Indian tribe to fight the United States Army, the so-called "Ghost Dance," with the leadership of the Cubists, who found brand-new things to do with surfaces and paint. He didn't say so, but he had already done this. And, thus directed, I reached a conclusion he must have reached.

But my thesis was rejected by the department,

as both grandiose and non-anthropological. And I
was out of time and money, and I accepted a job in
what was then arguably the most prosperous and
compassionate socialist state in history, the General
Electric Company in Schenectady, New York.

For whatever it may be worth, and it may be
worth no more than "a pitcher of warm spit," as we
used to say in the Army: The leadership of both the
Ghost Dance and the Cubist movement had these
elements in common:

1. A charismatic, gifted leader who described cul-
 tural changes which should be made;
2. Two or more respected citizens who testified
 that this leader was not a lunatic, but was well
 worth listening to;
3. A glib, personable explainer, who told the gen-
 eral public what the leader was up to, why he
 was so wonderful, and so on, day after day.

Turns out that such a table of organization
worked pretty well for Adolf Hitler, too, and
maybe for Robert Maynard Hutchins, when he

turned this place inside out and upside down sixty
years ago.

I was in Chicago a couple of years back on busi-
ness, and visited my old department. Professor Sol
Tax was the only teacher from my time still on the
job. I asked after some of my old classmates, kib-
butzniks whose theses had been acceptable. One,
he said, was practicing urban anthropology in Bos-
ton, and I allowed as how I had worked for a couple
of years in an ad agency there.

I told him what I've told you, how much I owed
Dr. Z. I didn't comment on Z's having been low
man on the department's totem pole, the Mespou-
lets. I would be very happy, incidentally, if that
word, "Mespoulets," became a part of academic
conversations, identifying that faculty member
stuck with being mentor to all the nobodies going
nowhere. In ad agencies it is common to start out
in the mail room. On faculties it is common to start
out as a Mespoulets.

Use a new word three times in conversation,
I read in *Reader's Digest* when I was a juvenile
delinquent, and it becomes a permanent part of

your vocabulary. Dr. Z was a Mespoulets, and
died without having risen above that rank. Sol
Tax may have been a Mespoulets at one time, but
he certainly wasn't one when I got here. I find it
hard to believe that the head of the department,
Dr. Robert Redfield, who made his reputation, and
the department's reputation, too, with an extended
essay called "The Folk Society," had ever been a
Mespoulets. There: that's three times, I think.

Dr. Tax, recalling the department's dead and
gone Mespoulets of long ago, said that Dr. Z had
written well about the controversial Native Ameri-
can religion, the Peyote Cult.

So far as Dr. Tax was aware, Dr. Z hadn't done
much writing since then. Only those of us who took
Z's freestyle summer course were aware of the scale
of the ambitions of our mentor. Each seminar, we
came to realize, was an airing and testing of ideas
in a chapter of a book about the human condition
he was writing or planned to write. I didn't share
that information with Dr. Tax, but I did ask him if
he had the address of my dead mentor's longtime
widow. He did.

She had long since remarried. I wrote to her,
wanting to tell her how stimulating I had found
her first husband, and how useful his wide-ranging
speculations had been to me in my career in fiction.
I must have reminded her of utterly ghastly unhap-
piness which she had hoped to put behind her. We
had never met, and never will meet, for there was
no reply.

If there had been one, I would have asked her if
he got any of his big ideas on paper, and where, if
anywhere, some pages were. Ah me.

Long term, I am as indebted to the head of the
department in my day, Dr. Robert Redfield, as I
am to its Mespoulets. Dostoyevsky suggested that
one sacred memory from childhood was perhaps
the best education. I say to you that one plausible,
romantic theory about humanity is perhaps the best
prize you can take away from a university. And Dr.
Redfield's theory of the Folk Society was that for
me. It has been the starting point for my politics,
such as they are.

My politics in a nutshell: let's stop giving cor-
porations and newfangled contraptions what they

need, and get back to giving human beings what
we need.

Long before I got here, all theories of cultural
evolution had been proposed and discarded, for
want of evidence to support them. Cultures were
not describable, predictable rungs on a ladder
societies were bound to climb, from polytheism to
monotheism, for example, and so on.

But Dr. Redfield said, in effect, and I condense
and paraphrase or worse: "Wait a minute. I think
I can describe in some detail one stage many,
many societies have reached or left behind, neither
higher or lower than any other." It might be worth
thinking about because it was or had been so com-
mon. Dr. Redfield's course in the Folk Society,
which he gave every year, was enormously popu-
lar, drawing auditors from all over the university.
Is his theory much discussed here or anywhere
nowadays?

A Folk Society, he said, was a relatively small
number of persons bonded by kinship and a com-
mon history of some duration, with a territory
uncontested or easily defended, and sufficiently

isolated so as to be little influenced by the cultures
of other societies.

There can't be many such societies nowadays.
There were still quite a few when I first came here.
I recall the testimony of some people who had lived
in one to the effect that the isolation, the like-mind-
edness, the routines and so on were suffocating.

I can believe it. I myself never visited one,
unless you want to count the anthropology depart-
ment itself.

But I had certainly read about a lot of them in the
library here. It seemed to me that they, because of
their simplicity and isolation, might be regarded as
petri dishes in which human beings might demon-
strate certain apparently basic human needs other
than food, shelter, clothing, and sex. For want of
a better word, I will call such needs spiritual, by
which I mean only that they are invisible, un-smell-
able, inaudible, intangible, and inedible.

Was it possible, I wondered, that certain features
common to all of them not only revealed spiritual
needs of all human beings, including those of us
in this auditorium? Might not those features also

show us methods for satisfying those needs, theatrical performances, if you will, which human beings, by their nature, can ill-afford to do without?

I think of the British Navy, whose sailors, although filling the world's oceans, felt lousy all the time, until they started sucking limes. A vitamin deficiency, of course! And here we are in the post-industrial, post–Cold War whatchamacallit, feeling lousy all the time. We get all the minerals and vitamins we need. Is it conceivable that we are suffering from a cultural deficiency which we can remedy? Friends and neighbors, I say YES to that:

Let's give everybody a totem at birth. What proof do I have that even highly educated people need nonsensical, arbitrary symbols which will relate them to other people and the Earth and the Universe? I am a Scorpio. Would those of you who are also Scorpios please hold up your hands? Lookee there! Dostoyevsky was one of us!

Yes, and let's find a way to get ourselves and others extended families again. A husband and a wife and some kids aren't a family, any more than a Diet Pepsi and three Oreos is a breakfast. Twenty, thirty, forty

people—that's a family. Marriages are all busting up. Why? Mates are saying to each other, because they're human, "You're not enough people for me."

Yes, and let's make sure every American gets a puberty ceremony, an impressive welcome to the rights and duties of grown-ups. As matters now stand, only practicing Jews get those. The only way the rest of us can feel like grown-ups is to get pregnant or get somebody else pregnant or commit a felony or go to war and then come back again.

I only want to say in closing that it's nice to be home again.

9
HOW I LEARNED FROM
A TEACHER WHAT ARTISTS DO

Syracuse University, Syracuse, New York,
May 8, 1994

And how we can do it!

There are three things that I very much want to say
in this brief hail and farewell. They are things which
haven't been said enough to you freshly minted
graduates nor to your parents or guardians, nor to
me, nor to your teachers. I will say these in the body
of my speech, I'm just setting you up for this.

First, I will say thank you. Second, I will say I
am truly sorry—now that is the striking novelty
among the three. We live in a time when nobody
ever seems to apologize for anything; they just

weep and raise hell on the *Oprah Winfrey Show*. The third thing I want to say to you at some point— probably close to the end—is, "We love you." Now if I fail to say any of those three things in the body of this great speech, hold up your hands, and I will remedy the deficiency.

And I'm going to ask you to hold up your hands this early in the proceedings for another reason. I first declare to you that the most wonderful thing, the most valuable thing you can get from an education is this—the memory of one person who could really teach, whose lessons made life and yourselves much more interesting and full of possibilities than you had previously supposed possible. I ask this of everyone here, including all of us up here on the platform—How many of us, how many of you, had such a teacher? Kindergarten counts. Please hold up your hands. Hurry. You may want to remember the name of that great teacher.

I thank you for being educated. There, I've thanked you now; that way I don't have to speak to a bunch of nincompoops. For you freshly minted college graduates, this is a puberty ceremony long

overdue. We, whose principal achievement is that we are older than you, have to acknowledge at last that you are grown-ups, too. There are old poops possibly among us on this very day who will say that you are not grown-ups until you have somehow survived, as they have, some famous calamity—the Great Depression, World War II, Vietnam, whatever. Storytellers are responsible for this destructive, not to say suicidal, myth. Again and again in stories, after some terrible mess, the character is able to say at last, "Today, I am a woman; today I am a man. The end."

I apologize. I said I would apologize; I apologize now. I apologize because of the terrible mess the planet is in. But it has always been a mess. There have never been any "Good Old Days," there have just been days. And as I say to my grandchildren, "Don't look at me. I just got here myself."

So you know what I'm going to do? I declare everybody here a member of Generation A. Tomorrow is another day for all of us.

Having said that, I have made us, for a few hours at least, what most of us do not have and

what we need so desperately—I have made us
an extended family, one for all and all for one. A
husband, a wife, and some kids is not a family; it's
a terribly vulnerable survival unit. Now those of
you who get married or are married, when you
fight with your spouse, what each of you will be
saying to the other one actually is, "You're not
enough people. You're only one person. I should
have hundreds of people around."

Now, I've made us an extended family. Does
our family have a flag? Well, you bet. It's a big
orange rectangle. Orange is a very good color
and maybe the best one. It's full of vitamin C and
cheerful associations, if one could forget the trou-
bles in Ireland.

Now this gathering is a work of art. The teacher
whose name I mentioned when we all remembered
good teachers asked me one time, "What is it art-
ists do?" And I mumbled something. "They do
two things," he said. "First, they admit they can't
straighten out the whole universe. And then sec-
ond, they make at least one little part of it exactly
as it should be. A blob of clay, a square of canvas, a

piece of paper, or whatever." We have all worked so hard and well to make these moments and this place exactly what it should be.

As I have told you, I had a bad uncle named Dan, who said a male can't be a man unless he'd gone to war. But I had a good uncle named Alex, who said, when life was most agreeable—and it could be just a pitcher of lemonade in the shade—he would say, "If this isn't nice, what is?" So I say that about what we have achieved here right now. If he hadn't said that so regularly, maybe five or six times a month, we might not have paused to notice how rewarding life can be sometimes. Perhaps my good Uncle Alex will live on in some of you members of this graduating class, if, in the future, you will pause to say out loud every so often, "If this isn't nice, what is?"

Now, my time is up and I haven't even inspired you with heroic tales of the past—Teddy Roosevelt's cavalry charge up San Juan Hill, Desert Storm— nor given you visions of a glorious future—computer programs, interactive TV, the information superhighway, speed the day. I spent too much time celebrating this very moment and place—once the

future we dreamed of so long ago. This is it. We're here. How the heck did we do it?

A neighbor of mine, I hired him—he was a handyman—to build an "L" on my house where I could write. He did the whole damn thing—he built the foundation, and then the side walls and the roof. He did it all by himself. And when it was all done, he stood back and he said, "How the hell did I ever do that?" How the hell did we ever do this? We did it! And if this isn't nice, what is?

There was one thing I forgot to say, and I promised I would say, and that is, "We love you. We really do."

10
DON'T FORGET WHERE
YOU COME FROM

Butler University, Indianapolis, Indiana,
May 11, 1996

Vonnegut celebrates his own hometown, and hopes
that some graduates will become the kind of "saints"
who make life worthwhile.

Hello, and congratulations.

And thank you. You have made our nation stronger and more admirable by becoming educated at great expense.

At great expense, God knows, God knows.

If I had it to do all over, I would choose to grow up again at Forty-fourth Street and North Illinois in Indianapolis, Indiana. I would be born again in

one of this city's hospitals, again be a product of its public schools.

I would again take courses in bacteriology and quantitative analysis in the summer school of Butler University.

It was all here for me, just as it has all been here for you: the best and the worst of civilization, if right here you can find music, finance, government, architecture, painting and sculpture, history, medicine, athletics, and books, books, books, and science.

And role models and teachers.

People so smart you can't believe it, and people so dumb you can't believe it.

People so nice you can't believe it, and people so mean you can't believe it.

The funniest wise man in the world when I was growing up wasn't in London or Paris or New York City. He was here in Indianapolis. His name was Kin Hubbard, and he wrote an elegant joke a day for the *Indianapolis News* under the pen name "Abe Martin."

Kin Hubbard said he didn't know anybody who'd be willing to work for what he was really worth.

He was funnier and wiser than David Letterman.

I went to high school with at least thirty people who were as funny as David Letterman.

There's something about the air here.

One woman I went to high school with, Madeline Pugh, became the head writer on the *I Love Lucy* show.

Mr. Letterman grew up here, in what show business people, which now includes our best-known politicians and so-called journalists, often call "flyover country."

We are somewhere between television cameras in Washington, DC, and New York, and Los Angeles.

Please join me in saying to the undersides of their airplanes, "Go to hell."

The greatest of American presidents, Abraham Lincoln, came from Kentucky, Indiana, and Illinois.

Arguably the greatest poet and the greatest playwright of this century, T. S. Eliot and Tennessee Williams, came from St. Louis.

Arguably the greatest friend the working people in this country ever had, Eugene Debs, was from Terre Haute.

He said, "As long as there is a lower class I am in it, as long as there is a criminal class I am of it, as long as there is a soul in prison I am not free."

It used to be admirable for Americans to talk that way.

Will some educated person here tell me what went wrong?

What I'm saying is that this is very fertile soil here. I'm not talking about corn and pigs.

I'm talking about growing important souls and intellects.

The people I choose to celebrate today, though, aren't those Middle Westerners who became world famous.

Do you know, incidentally, that one of the most impossibly sophisticated, worldly persons ever to grace the planet, the composer and lyricist Cole Porter, the toast of New York and London and Paris, came from Pee-ru, Indiana?

Pee-ru, for heavens' sakes.

Can you beat it? How close is that to Brazil and Kokomo?

The people I admire the heck out of today are those who built cities like this, with universities like this one, with symphony halls like that one, with art museums like the one over there somewhere, with libraries in every neighborhood. And the churches and hospitals. And the factories and stores. Utopia.

I'm talking to TV celebrities in airplanes again:
Hey, you monstrously overpaid electronic twerps:
"Down here" is where the real lives are led.
"Down here" is where the real work gets done.
The airplane itself was invented in Ohio.
So was Alcoholics Anonymous. The rear-view mirror.

Yes, and wonderful dancers all over the world
have come or will come from Butler University in
Naptown. Are some of them here?

Some of you won't stay home. But please don't
forget where you came from. I never did.

Notice when you're happy, and know when
you've got enough.

As for throwing money at problems: that's what
money is for.

My Uncle Alex Vonnegut, an insurance salesman
who lived at 5033 North Pennsylvania, taught me
something very important. He said that when things
are going really well we should be sure to notice it.
He was talking about very simple occasions, not
great victories. Maybe drinking lemonade under
a shade tree, or smelling the aroma of a bakery, or
fishing, or listening to music coming from a concert

hall while standing in the dark outside, or, dare I say, after a kiss. He told me that it was important at such times to say out loud, "If this isn't nice, what is?"

Uncle Alex, who is buried in Crown Hill along with James Whitcomb Riley, and my sister, and my parents, and my grandparents, and my great-grandparents, and John Dillinger, thought it was a terrible waste to be happy and not notice it.

So do I.

You have been called "Generation X."

You're as much Generation A as Adam and Eve were.

As I read the book of Genesis, God didn't give Adam and Eve a whole planet.

He gave them a manageable piece of property, for the sake of discussion let's say two hundred acres.

I suggest to you Adams and Eves that you set as your goals the putting of some small part of the planet into something like safe and sane and decent order.

There's a lot of cleaning up to do.

There's a lot of rebuilding to do, both spiritual and physical.

And, again, there's going to be a lot of happiness. Don't forget to notice!

11
WHY SOCIAL JUSTICE
DOES MORE THAN ART TO
NOURISH THE AMERICAN DREAM

The State University of New York at Albany,

May 20, 1972

Vonnegut urges us to touch one another and become a family, taking care of each other as families do, and spend more money on schools, hospitals, and Ferris wheels.

It is nice of you to have me here.

I have been asked to make an announcement by the management: If anyone cheated in the process of getting a degree, now is the time to confess it and leave quietly. If you don't confess it now, you will be haunted by bogeymen for the rest of your lives—and by a very angry Santa Claus.

143

I never graduated from college, but I am sick about things I did in high school. I, too, was invited to confess. And did I? No. That is one of the reasons I have heebie-jeebies all the time.

Another reason I have the heebie-jeebies is that I am almost sure we have been invaded by flying saucer creatures from the planet Pluto. That will be the big news in this speech, I think—about the invasion from Pluto and what Earthlings can do about it. But I'd like to save that for a little later on.

※

My brother works here. He used to work in a bloomer factory. It was a very good job. He was pulling down twenty-five thousand a year.

That isn't really true. I just like that joke so much. Actually my brother is a scientist, and always has been—and an Earthling, too, as far as I know.

He works in your department of Atmospheric Sciences. You mustn't picket him or blow him up. Dr. Bernard Vonnegut is not in war work. He is trying to find peace-time uses for thunder and lightning. I made sure he had tenure before I agreed to speak.

Bernard and I used to work for General Electric over in Schenectady. I have worked for several large corporations in my life. This is the first time I have knowingly worked for Standard Oil.

※

I am an exemplar. I would not have been invited here, if I were not exemplary. I am in *Who's Who*. I am costing about what a used 1968 Volkswagen would cost—with a busted tape deck and good rubber all around.

I will show you today what Diogenes had such trouble finding—an honest man. I am perhaps the second honest man ever to come to Albany. My brother was the first. He moved in from Delmar about four months ago. He can tell you the truth about the sciences, which are killing us all. I will tell you the truth about the arts, which would like to drive us crazy.

You may have been told at the great institution of higher learning that the arts are good for everybody—or at any rate have no harmful side effects. That isn't true. One of the principal uses of the arts in this and many other modern countries is to confuse the uneducated and the powerless and the poor.

I am talking about *expensive* arts now, tremendously official arts—and not the little tunes and poems and pictures and stories which the downtrodden select or create for their own amusement.

I am talking about the arts which are supported by dictators and social climbers and multimillionaires.

I have heard powerful men on both sides of the Iron Curtain praising the arts. I have been in their museums and concert balls. I have seen the common people attempting to appreciate the art treasures said to be worth hundreds of thousands of dollars or rubles or what have you. The common people always look waterlogged. They seem to have double pneumonia. They swoon with apathy.

This is what is *supposed* to happen.

The purpose of the museums and concert halls and theaters and public statuary and so on is to persuade the common people that they are unworthy of holding power or making big money—because their minds and spirits are inferior.

Proof of their inferiority is the fact that they are incapable of appreciating great art.

✽

The rich and powerful are even more bored by the arts than the common people. One has only to attend the opera in any country but Italy to know this is so.

But they have to pretend to appreciate the arts in order to demonstrate their natural superiority, since they can scarcely demonstrate it in any other way. And I pity them. I am a compassionate man. How much fun can it be, really, to pretend to love Rembrandt's *Aristotle Contemplating a Bust of Homer* day in and day out, year in and year out? How much fun can it be to pretend to love the German opera—or *War and Peace*, which you haven't read, even though you're a Russian?

How much fun can it be, day in and day out, to pretend to admire the Leaning Tower of Pisa or the Albany Mall?

✽

I assume most of you are sufficiently familiar with modern art history to know what I mean by "the Albany Mall." Then again, perhaps architecture isn't thought of as being one of the fine arts at the State University of New York at Albany.

That would certainly be understandable. My
brother has gunports instead of windows in his
laboratory. He turned on his Bunsen burner, and
Pepsi-Cola came out.

Be that as it may: I like the fine arts all right,
but I doubt that they are any finer than a lot of
other human games. And I deny most bitterly that
persons claiming to love the fine arts are neces-
sarily fine people. The emperor Nero was a patron
of the arts. So was Herman Goering. So were so
many of the American economic robber barons
who cut the guts out of what was left of the Amer-
ican dream after the Civil War.

*

There is some small chance, I suppose, that some
works of art are closer to God or Truth or what
have you than some other things which men have
made. I am a Unitarian, so I wouldn't know. I
have no handles on God or Truth.

I *do* know something about the American
dream, since that is what brought my ancestors
from Germany to Indiana so long ago. And I can
name things men and women have done which are

closer to the American dream than any book or statue or painting or building or song. These are the acts of social justice.

*

We have plenty of art, and important art, too. I will guess that one American in twenty has a love for the arts which is joyful and natural and genuine. I am one of those persons, and had to get out of Indianapolis on that account.

And that tiny part of our population which appreciates the arts is well taken care of, is often appalled by how much good stuff there is to read and see and listen to. We have plenty of art in America.

It is social justice which is in gruesomely short supply.

*

Can the arts distract some people from social justice? Yes—they can. Consider the case of Thomas Jefferson, our third president, the author of our Declaration of Independence. He died on the Fourth of July, by the way. Nobody ever wrote more eloquently about freedom and fair play and the natural rights of every human being than Jefferson.

He was also fond of architecture and the pleasant things which can happen in well-designed dwellings when labor is cheap and tractable. So he kept human slaves until he was an old man. He let them go at last, but he was old by then.

Let us forgive Thomas Jefferson. He had a weakness for the finer things in life. A lot of us do. What's wrong with a little slavery?

<div align="center">✻</div>

Dear friends—I have told you that the arts often play an insidious part in class warfare.

And you have said to yourselves perhaps, "Well—this is fairly interesting, maybe, but it's irrelevant. Our present king doesn't even pretend to be interested in the arts. Neither do his buddies Bebe Rebosa and John Mitchell and Billy Graham and so on."

The point is well taken. You may have noticed that more and more people are rising to the top of our society who are not only indifferent to the arts, but to jokes and cheerful sex, and to all sorts of human playfulness. I have noticed this, too. And this is what has led me to believe that flying saucer creatures from Pluto have invaded us.

Pluto is a suspicious and prideful and secretive and warlike planet, with a technology far in advance of our own. My guess is that Plutonians began to arrive and reproduce and hold jobs in our government just as the Second World War was ending. Our last three presidents may have been Plutonians. Most of them, however, are in the Pentagon.

We would perhaps welcome them, if it weren't for their humorlessness and pitilessness, and their blather about national honor—and for their love of war.

Also they are not respectful of the Constitution of the United States of America, the most exuberant work of art in the history of this planet. So let us ask ourselves today, at this long-overdue puberty ceremony: "What can Earthlings do?"

He can't beat the Plutonians militarily. They have all the weapons. A Plutonian, almost by definition, is a person with a weapon. Governor Wallace was shot by a Plutonian.

We could try to beat them politically. But Plutonians engage in power politics and nothing but power politics from junior high school on. What Earthling could do that? Let us face it: an Earthling's sense of humor and fascination with sex

makes it impossible for him or her to concentrate
seriously on anything, even his or her survival, for
more than an hour at a time.

Our best hope, it seems to me, lies in our band-
ing together in order to be proud of being Earth-
lings. The Plutonians, like all invaders, want the
natives to be ashamed of their own ideals and
dreams. We might choose as our motto: "Earth-
lings are beautiful."

Or we might start more modestly with: "Ameri-
cans are beautiful." We could go planetary later
on. Americans aren't beautiful now, of course,
because of the Plutonians among us. But there is a
chance that we can change that now.

<p style="text-align:center">✻</p>

I propose a great adventure to you. That is some-
thing every good graduation speaker is expected
to do. When I graduated from high school, the
speaker told us about the great adventures we
could have in science—especially in plastics and
polarized light. I wound up in the infantry in-
stead. Almost everybody did.

I propose a better adventure than polarized light
or the infantry or plastics or the arts or the explo-

ration of outer space or the conquest of cancer or athlete's foot. I think you should devote your lives to creating something which this planet has never had. The planet will die, if it doesn't get it now.

You must create an American people. There never has been one. You must create one now. We must create one now. This is a matter of life or death.

*

When I spoke of the Plutonians and the Earthlings, I was of course alluding to the murderous half and the healing half of every American I have ever known. If I don't mention the good and evil in foreigners, that is because I don't know doodley-poop about foreigners. I've seldom been far from home. Get a world traveler next time.

One thing I have noticed, though, staying close to home, is that those who rule us, nearly two-hundred years after the signing of the Declaration of Independence, do not want an American people to be born. To them, our hatred for one another, our unwillingness to touch one another, have been votes in the ballot box and money in the bank.

I will tell you an embarrassing story about myself, about my own one-hundred-per-cent-American

unwillingness to touch another human being, even a close relative. I adopted a boy when he was fourteen. He was my nephew. When he was twenty-one, I congratulated him on being a man, and he said to me, "Do you know you have never hugged me?"

What a hell of a thing to say.

❖

I didn't want him to think I was a homosexual.

❖

At the very core of my American education was a dread of any gesture which might be interpreted by the football coach as being even vaguely homosexual. The safest thing to do was to never touch anybody— not even Mom. Or maybe especially not Mom.

I was also taught that American men seldom cry, except when the flag goes by. I couldn't even cry when that boy told me I had never hugged him. I was also taught to fear words. Some words, I was taught, could never be spoken at an assembly like this without making us all feel ashamed and diseased. They had to do with sex and excretion. I was taught the American fear of germs, which is more frantic than the worst nightmare Louis Pasteur

ever had. But the fear of germs was extended to strangers, too. My parents and my hygiene teacher told me, in effect, "Beware of strangers or anything touched by strangers. Or you're liable to get syphilis or leprosy or the bubonic plague."

I look back on all the taboos that I was taught, that everybody was taught, and I see now that they were parts of a great swindle. Their purpose was to make Americans afraid to get close to one another—to organize.

It was even taboo to discuss the American economic system and its bizarre methods of disturbing wealth. I learned that at my mother's knee. God rest her soul. God rest her knee. She taught me never to say anything impolite about the neighborhood millionaire. She didn't even want me to wonder out loud how the hell he ever got to control that much wealth.

*

We must learn to deal with one another more frankly and openly, even humorously. But, more important than that, we must learn to touch. If we are to become a strong and decent people, we must

become cousins now—eccentric cousins maybe, but cousins all the same. Blood is thicker than water. Let us learn from the Mafia. It is time, incidentally, that the white people in this country acknowledged that the so-called black people are actually blood relatives of theirs. This is easily proved.

But this is no time to marvel and cackle over family trees. This is a time for us to become excited about being members of the family of man.

Does anyone have nerve enough to touch a stranger near him or her now? Even an old person? Ambulances are waiting outside. First aid stations have been set up in white nylon tents, in case you need oxygen or want to want to wash your hands in Lysol.

If an American people is to be born during the tragedy of the war in Vietnam, it is going to have to be a personal, visceral adventure.

I do not apologize for making this suggestion.

*

We must become a family in order to take care of one another the way families do. Now, nearly two hundred years after the signing of the Declaration of Independence, written by a man who owned human

slaves, I think we understand that our politicians
and millionaires can do very little for us, except to
take our money. There are sound reasons for this,
I'm sure. I mean to study economics some day.

Meanwhile, we must love one another and care for
one another as best we can, and we must organize.
You, our new generation of adults, must organize us.

And if our government persists in being as
wrong-headed as it is today, you must threaten it
with the only effective weapon the Earthlings have
against the Plutonians, which is a general strike.

*

I have tried to preach pacifism today. If I were the
White House preacher, I would try to make a Quak-
er out of Richard M. Nixon. That is how crazy I am.

Our history teaches us that we need not fear
pacifism. It will not leave our nation defenseless.
I was raised to be a pacifist, and so were most
people my age. In the public schools of Indianapo-
lis and in the public schools of all over the land,
people my age were instructed when young to jeer
at the nations of Europe for maintaining enor-
mous standing armies, for wasting their substance
on weapons and allowing generals and admirals to

help decide what the nations would do next, where the energy and the money and people would go.

I learned my contempt for the military at the same place I learned to fear germ-laden strangers and symptoms of homosexuality and so on—in the public schools. "Every cloud has a silver lining," as they say.

Well—all those yellow-bellied pacifists produced by the American public school system in the nineteen-thirties became a harrowingly effective army in the early forties, when we got into a war which seemed just.

*

As for preparing this country against an attack from anti-missile anti-missile anti-missiles. By developing an anti-missile anti-missile anti-missile anti-missile, I may be in the minority, but I think the American people should spend the money on hospitals and housing and schools and Ferris wheels instead.

Thank you, and good luck.

12
HOW TO BE A WISE GUY OR A WISE GIRL

Southampton College, Southampton, New York, June 7,
1981

Be aware, notice small things, challenge the status
quo and save countless lives, like Vonnegut's hero, Ignaz
Semmelweiss, did in Vienna. "Be honorable!"

This speech conforms to the methods recommend-
ed by the United States Army Manual on how
to teach. You tell people what you're going to tell
them. Then you tell them, then you tell them what
you told them.

Now we'll first discuss honorable behavior, es-
pecially in peacetime, and we'll then comment on
the information revolution—the astonishing fact
that human beings can actually know what they're

talking about in case they want to try it. From
there, I will go on to recommend to those gradu-
ating from colleges everywhere in the world this
spring that their hero be Ignaz Semmelweis.

You may laugh at such a name for a hero, but
you will become most respectful, I promise you,
when I tell you how and why he died.

After I describe Ignaz Semmelweis a little, I
will ask if he might not represent the next stage of
human evolution. I will conclude that he had bet-
ter be. If he doesn't represent what we're going to
become next, then life is all over for us and for the
cockroaches and the dandelions too.

I will give you a hint about him. He saved the
lives of many women and children. If we continue
on our present course there will be less and less of
that going on. OK.

Now we come to the main body of the speech,
which is an amplification of the first part. See how
memorable it all becomes. No wonder we have the
greatest Army in the world. Honor. I have always
wanted to be honorable. All of you want to be
honorable too, I'm sure.

A lot of the talk about honor in the past has had to do with behavior on the battlefield. An honorable man holds his country's flag high even though he is as full of arrows as St. Sebastian. An honorable little drummer boy drums and drums and drums rat-a-tattat, rat-a-tat-tat till he has his little head blown off.

General Haig should really be here to talk about that sort of honor. I was only a corporal. Modern weapons, of course, have made that sort of honor even scarier than it used to be.

A person in control of missiles and nuclear warheads could behave so honorably as to get everybody killed. The whole planet could become like the head of the brave little drummer boy rolling off into a ditch somewhere.

So I will limit my discussion to honorable behavior in peacetime situations. In peacetime it is honorable to tell the truth to those who deserve to hear it.

You guarantee that you are telling the truth by saying I give my word of honor that such and such is true. I have never knowingly lied, having said first I give my word of honor. So I now give

you my word of honor that it is a courageous and
honorable and beautiful thing you have done to
become college graduates.

I give you my word of honor that we love you
and need you. We love you simply because you are
of our species. You have been born. That is enough.

We need you because we hope to survive as a
species, and you are in possession of or can get pos-
session of solid information which, properly under-
stood and put to use, can save us as a species.

I give you my word of honor as the adult ver-
sion of "cross my heart and hope to die." We are
drawing ever closer to Ignaz Semmelweis, in case
you're wondering what on earth happened to him.
Just be patient. Most of you, if not all of you, feel
inadequately educated. That is an ordinary feeling
for a member of our species. One of the most bril-
liant human beings of all times, George Bernard
Shaw, said on his 75th birthday or so that he knew
enough at last to become a mediocre office boy.
He died in 1950, by the way, when I was 28, about
10 years before most of you were born.

He would envy you now. He would envy your

youth, surely. Perhaps you all know what he said
about youth, that it was a shame to waste it on
the young.

But he would be even greedier for the solid
information which you have or can get about the
nature of the universe, about time and space and
matter, about your own bodies and brains, about
the resources and vulnerabilities of our planet,
about how all sorts of human beings actually talk
and feel and live.

This is the information revolution I promised
to tell you about. We have taken it very badly so
far. Information seems to be getting in the way all
the time. Human beings have had to guess about
almost everything for the past million years or so.
Our most enthralling and sometimes terrifying
guesses are the leading characters in our history
books. Should I name two of them? Aristotle and
Hitler. One good guesser and one bad one.

If you haven't heard of them by now, this is a
bust of a graduation. And the masses of humanity
having no solid information have had little choice
but to believe this guesser or that one. Russians

who didn't think much of the guesses of Ivan the Terrible, for example, were likely to have their hats nailed to their heads.

Let us acknowledge, though, that persuasive guessers, even Ivan the Terrible, now a hero in the Soviet Union, have given us courage to endure extraordinary ordeals which we had no way of understanding. Crop failures, wars, plagues, eruptions of volcanoes, babies being born dead—they gave us the illusion that bad luck and good luck were understandable and could somehow be dealt with intelligently and effectively.

Without that illusion, we would all have surrendered long ago. The guessers, in fact, knew no more than the common people and sometimes less. The important thing was that somebody gave us the illusion that we're in control of our destinies.

Persuasive guessing has been at the core of leadership for so long for all of human experience so far that it is wholly unsurprising that most of the leaders of this planet, in spite of all the information that is suddenly ours, want the guessing to go on.

It is now their turn to guess and guess and be listened to. Some of the loudest, most proudly ignorant guessing in the world is going on in Washington today. Our leaders are sick of all the solid information that has been dumped on humanity by research and scholarship and investigative reporting.

They think that the whole country is sick of it, and they could be right. It isn't the gold standard that they want to put us back on; they want something even more basic than that. They want to put us back on the snake-oil standard again

Loaded pistols are good for people unless they're in prisons or lunatic asylums. That's correct. Millions spent on public health are inflationary. That's correct. Billions spent on weapons will bring inflation down. That's correct. Dictatorships to the right are much closer to American ideals than dictatorships to the left. That's correct. The more hydrogen bomb warheads we have all set to go off at a moment's notice, the safer humanity is, the better the world our grandchildren will inherit. That's correct.

Industrial wastes and especially those which are radioactive hardly ever hurt anybody, so everybody should shut up about them. That's correct.

Industries should be allowed to do whatever they want to do. Bribe, wreck the environment just a little, fix prices, screw dumb customers, put a stop to competition and raid the Treasury in case they grow broke. That's correct. That's for enterprise. That's correct.

The poor have done something very wrong or they wouldn't be poor, so their children should pay the consequences. That's correct. The United States of America cannot be expected to look after its people. That's correct. The free market will do that. That's correct. The free market is an automatic system of justice. That's correct.

And if you actually remember one-tenth of what you've learned here, you will not be welcome in Washington, DC. I know a couple of bright seventh graders who would not be welcomed in Washington, DC. Do you remember those doctors a few months back who got together and announced that it was a simple, clear medical fact that we could not survive

even a moderate attack by hydrogen bombs? They were not welcome in Washington, DC.

Even if we fired the first salvo of hydrogen weapons and the enemy never fired back, the poisons released would probably kill the whole planet by and by.

What is the response in Washington? They guess otherwise. What good is an education? The boisterous guessers are still in charge—the haters of information. And the guessers are almost all highly educated people, think of that. They have had to throw away their education; even Harvard or Yale education.

If they didn't do that, there is no way their noninhibited guessing could go on and on and on. Please, don't you do that. And I give you something to cling to; for if you make use of the vast fund of knowledge now available to educated persons, you are going to be lonesome as hell. The guessers outnumber you and now I have to guess about 10 to 1.

The thing I give you to cling to is a poor thing, actually. Not much better than nothing, and maybe it's a little worse than nothing. I've already given

it to you. It is the idea of a truly modern hero. It is
the bare bones of the life of Ignaz Semmelweis. My
hero is Ignaz Semmelweis. You may be wondering
if I'm going to make you say that out loud again.
No, I'm not, you've heard it for the last time.

He was born in Budapest in 1818. His life over-
lapped with that of my grandfather and with that of
your great-grandfathers and it may seem a long time
ago to you, but actually he lived only yesterday.

He became an obstetrician, which should make
him modern hero enough. He devoted his life to
the health of babies and mothers. We could use
more heroes like that. There's damn little caring
for mothers or babies or old people or anybody
physically or economically weak these days as we
become ever more industrialized and militarized
with the guessers in charge.

I have said to you how new all this information
is. It is so new that the idea that many diseases are
caused by germs is only about 120 years old.

The house I own out here in Sagaponack is
twice that old. I don't know how they lived long
enough to finish it. I mean the germ theory is

really recent. When my father was a little boy,
Louis Pasteur was still alive and still plenty con-
troversial. There were still plenty of high-powered
guessers who were furious at people that would
listen to him instead of to them. Yes, and Ignaz
Semmelweis also believed that germs could cause
diseases. He was horrified when he went to work
for a maternity hospital in Vienna, Austria, to find
out that one mother in 10 was dying of childbed
fever there.

These were poor people—rich people still had
their babies at home. Semmelweis observed hos-
pital routines, and began to suspect that doctors
were bringing the infection to the patients. He
noticed that the doctors often went directly from
dissecting corpses in the morgue to examining
mothers in the maternity ward. He suggested as
an experiment that the doctors wash their hands
before touching the mothers.

What could be more insulting. How dare he
make such a suggestion to his social superiors.
He was a nobody, he realized. He was from out
of town with no friends and protectors among the

Austrian nobility. But all that dying went on and
on and Semmelweis, having far less sense about
how to get along with others in this world than
you and I would have, kept on asking his col-
leagues to wash their hands.

They at last agreed to do this in a spirit of lam-
poonery, of satire, of scorn. How they must have
lathered and lathered and scrubbed and scrubbed
and cleaned under their fingernails. The dying
stopped—imagine that! The dying stopped. He
saved all those lives.

Subsequently, it might be said that he has saved
millions of lives—including quite possibly yours
and mine. What thanks did Semmelweis get from
the leaders of his profession in Viennese society,
guessers all? He was forced out of the hospital and
out of Austria itself, whose people he had served
so well. He finished his career in a provincial
hospital in Hungary. There he gave up on human-
ity, which is us, and our knowledge, which is now
yours, and on himself.

One day in the dissecting room, he took the
blade of a scalpel with which he had been cutting

up a corpse, and he stuck it on purpose into the palm of his hand. He died, as he knew he would, of blood poisoning soon afterward.

The guessers had had all the power. They had won again. Germs indeed. The guessers revealed something else about themselves too, which we should duly note today. They aren't really interested in saving lives. What matters to them is being listened to—as however ignorantly their guessing goes on and on and on. If there's anything they hate, it's a wise guy or a wise girl.

Be one anyway. Save our lives and your lives too. Be honorable. I thank you for your attention.

13
WHY YOU CAN'T STOP ME FROM SPEAKING ILL OF THOMAS JEFFERSON

The Indiana Civil Liberties Union
(now The American Civil Liberties Union of Indiana),
Indianapolis, Indiana,
September 16, 2000

Vonnegut tells why the Bill of Rights is "more than just a bunch of amendments," but protects our most important liberties—like freedom of speech, and a lot more. He supports the Second Amendment and explains how "man-killing devices and live ammunition" can best serve us.

There is something you are entitled to know about me—something I'm not proud to confess. This is it: I was born into a society as segregated as Biloxi, Mississippi, except for the drinking fountains and the buses. And I am the product of a lily-white

173

public high school in Indianapolis. It had a faculty
worthy of a university. Our teachers there, again
lily-white, weren't just teachers. They *were* their
subjects. Our chemistry teachers were first and
foremost chemists. Our physics teachers were first
and foremost physicists. Our teacher of ancient
history, who was Minnie Lloyd, should have been
wearing medals for all she did at the Battle of
Thermopylae. Our English teachers were very
commonly serious writers. One of mine, the late
Marguerite Young, went on to write the definitive
biography of Indiana's own Eugene Victor
Debs, the middle-class labor leader and socialist
candidate for President of the United States, who
died in 1926, when I was 4. Millions voted for
Debs when he ran for President.

I never met Debs, but I was old enough after
World War II to have lunch in this city with
another middle-class Indiana labor leader. He was
Powers Hapgood. Although he was a Harvard
graduate and from a well-to-do family of business
people, Powers Hapgood worked as a coal miner to
get close, both spiritually and physically, to those he

wished to help to help themselves. He then became
an officer in the CIO here in Indianapolis.

Not long after our lunch, there was some kind of
dust-up on a picket line, and he landed in court as
a witness. The judge, Judge Claycomb, in fact the
father of my Shortridge classmate Moon Claycomb,
knew of Hapgood's history, and interrupted the
proceedings to ask why such a privileged person
would spend his life as he had. And Powers Hap-
good replied: "Why, the Sermon on the Mount, sir."

And if I am asked why anybody should support
their local and national Civil Liberties Unions, I
will say that it takes a powerful private organiza-
tion to compel those who govern us to not violate
the crystal clear laws in the Bill of Rights, just as
we would not want them to drive when drunk or
park by a fireplug. Given the humane and fair and
merciful intent of the Bill of Rights, what I would
actually be saying, though, subliminally, is, "The
Sermon on the Mount, sir or madam."

If you don't know what the Sermon on the
Mount is, ask your kid's computer. If you don't
know what the laws in the Bill of Rights are, look

'em up, look 'em up. And yes, I know about the
Second Amendment, and I'm for it. It doesn't say
people who disagree with a president should shoot
him, which is what John Wilkes Booth and Lee
Harvey Oswald did. It says in effect that civil-
ians interested in playing with man-killing devices
and live ammunition can best serve the rest of us
in the National Guard, as long as they don't shoot
unarmed college students.[2]

To come back to my lily-white high school, which
had a daily paper. It had such a stunning faculty
because the Great Depression was going on, so
teaching was a plum job for some of the smartest
men in town. But even before the stock market crash
of 1929, when I was 7, it had great teachers because
teaching high school was virtually the only way bril-
liant and informed women could make effective use
of their warmth and intellectual enthusiasm and gift-
edness. Most of my best teachers were women and,
holy smokes, were they ever bright.

2 Four unarmed students at Kent State University were shot
and killed by Ohio National Guardsmen on May 4, 1970, while
protesting against the invasion of Cambodia.

Why were women barred then from so many jobs they now hold with distinction? Because of what was then believed to be a law of Nature, a Natural Law. Otherwise, why would Nature have made women such lousy fighters? Most of 'em, with a very few strikingly unattractive exceptions, couldn't fight their way out of a paper bag.

Why were there no African Americans in my high school?

African Americans had their own high school, of course. It was Crispus Attucks. And because of the peculiar name of our black high school, people of all colors in Indianapolis were unusual Americans for knowing who Crispus Attucks was. He was an African American free man, not a slave, who stopped a British bullet at the Boston Massacre in 1770, only six years before our nation became a beacon of liberty for the whole wide world. In one book of mine, I nicknamed Crispus Attucks High School "Innocent Bystander High."

Again: Why were there no African Americans in Shortridge High School? Because of what was then believed to be a law of Nature, a Natural Law. Nature

had obviously color-coded people for a reason. Otherwise, what the hell were all these different colors for?

And why was Thomas Jefferson, possibly the most beloved of our founding fathers after George Washington, able to write "all men are created equal," while meaning only white males, not women, God knows, and while owning slaves? Because of what was then believed to be a law of Nature. Jefferson's slaves were mortgaged, by the way. What a shame that you can no longer take the cleaning lady, along with the saxophone, down to the hock shop, if you're short on cash. Those were sure the good old days.

In quite a few ways though, it was still the good old days for white males when I was growing up. I could still feel superior, even in the view of law-enforcement agencies, to half my own race and one hundred percent of all the others. That was comforting! Not only that, but I could get away with all kinds of crap because I was from a good family. But that's another story.

In our all-white sandlot football games, I remember—"Jeffersonian games," you might call them—

the ad hoc captain of the side preparing to kick off
would call out. "Are you ready, Crispus Attucks?"
And the captain of the receivers would inevitably
reply, "We are ready, Ladywood."[3] Come to think
of it, that "Ladywood" business had an anti-Cath-
olic ring to it. Come to think of it, we were not only
male and white, but also Protestant. So that "Lady-
wood" insult was a kind of two-fer.

If I have offended some of you by speaking ill
of Thomas Jefferson, tough titty for you. I can say
anything I please, short of shouting "Fire!" if there
is no fire, because I am a citizen of the U.S.A. Your
government does not exist and should not exist in
order to keep you or anybody else, no matter what
color, no matter what race, no matter what religion,
from getting your damn fool feelings hurt.

If you found an official powerful enough and
dumb enough to actually shut me up about Thomas
Jefferson, the two of you would be hauled into
court, and the Indiana Civil Liberties Union would
make you both feel like something the cat drug in.

3 Ladywood was a Catholic girls' school in Indianapolis.

Which brings us to Saint Thomas Aquinas, a
great Italian theologian and philosopher who eight
hundred years ago perceived a hierarchy of laws
which human beings should obey. At the top were
God's Laws, from the Old and New Testaments, of
course. Below them were Natural Laws, the ways
Nature, obviously, to both Saint Thomas and Jef-
ferson, expected things to go. Lowest of all were
man's laws. If you think of laws arranged in that
order in a deck of cards, God's Laws would be the
aces, Nature's law would be the kings, and ACLU
lawyers, attempting to secure the civil rights of the
deuces and treys and even unpopular tens and jacks
in our society, would have nothing but pipsqueak
queens to play. I in fact once heard a man dis-
miss the Bill of Rights as "nothing but a bunch of
amendments." Chickenfeed, when compared with
God and Nature.

And indeed the unambiguous laws in the Bill
of Rights might as well have been chickenfeed, or
even chicken droppings, so cruelly spotty was their
enforcement until the start of the lifetimes of people
my age—people born in 1922. Only two years before

we were born were female citizens allowed to vote
and run for office. My Lord! And for many years
after that, until long after the end of World War II,
for Heaven's sakes, African American citizens of
both sexes were in many parts of the country, this
beacon of liberty, discouraged from voting by a
combination of technicalities and sheer terror. Don't
forget: nobody had ever been punished for lynching
one. "Nature red in tooth and claw."[4]

Who were and are the bleeding hearts who
fought and fight to make our governments, local,
state and federal, behave justly and mercifully and
respectfully toward all its citizens, no matter how
socially and politically powerless and unpopu-
lar they may be? I have an old and once-despised
name for them which may surprise you. They are
"Abolitionists." We are Abolitionists. Abolition of
what? Of human slavery. Such passions for human
rights as we have derive their strength from inher-
ited guilt about the unspeakably hideous crime on

4 "Nature red in tooth and claw" is a quote from Tennyson's poem
"In Memoriam A.H.H.," and refers to predatory animals baring
their teeth and claws with the blood of the prey they killed.

which so much of the early and even present wealth
of the whole of this nation, under God, is based,
the labor of kidnapped persons, of slaves. And
we tonight are also atoning as best we can for the
murders of brothers by brothers, so to speak, in our
Civil War. "Mine eyes have seen the glory of the
coming of the Lord. He is trampling out the vine-
yards where the grapes of wrath are stored."

What did *The Battle Hymn of the Republic* and
Uncle Tom's Cabin and Lincoln's Gettysburg
Address and all that have to do with our present
enthusiasm for women's rights? Not that much,
really. Women just got lucky this time.

14
DON'T DESPAIR IF YOU NEVER WENT TO COLLEGE!

On receiving the Carl Sandburg Award, Chicago, Illinois, October 12, 2001

The Indiana author celebrates some self-taught Midwestern-ers who made waves from sea to shining sea. As a young man, Vonnegut once considered becoming a labor organizer, and he admired and honored those who fought for the rights of wage earners everywhere. As a member of PEN International, he fought for the rights of writers around the world.[5]

We are America's Great Lakes people, her fresh-water people, not an oceanic but a continental peo-

5 The Carl Sandburg Literary Award, given by the Chicago Public Library Foundation, "honors an author whose significant body of work has enhanced the public's awareness of the written word."

185

ple. Whenever I swim in an ocean, I feel as though I am swimming in chicken soup.

I thank you for this honor, although it is a reminder that I am not nearly the passionate and effective artist Carl Sandburg was. And we are surely grateful for his fog which came in on little cat feet.[6] But tonight seems an apt occasion as well for celebrating what he and other American socialists did during the first half of the past century, with art, with eloquence, with organizing skills, to elevate the self-respect, the dignity, and political acumen of American wage earners, of our working class.

That wage earners, without social position or higher education or wealth, are of inferior intellect is surely belied by the fact that two of the most splendid writers and speakers on the deepest subjects in American history were self-taught workmen. I speak, of course, of Carl

6 Carl Sandburg's poem "Fog" was memorized and recited in many grade schools—at least all over the Midwest when we were growing up. Everyone knew it at least for a while. It was a favorite to recite in school poetry contests because it was so short! Fog / The fog comes / on little cat feet. / It sits looking / over harbor and city / on silent haunches / and then moves on.—DW

Sandburg of Illinois, and Abraham Lincoln, of
Kentucky, then Indiana, and finally Illinois.
Both, may I say, were continental, freshwater
people like ourselves.

Hooray for our team!

I know upper-class graduates of Yale University
who can't talk or write worth a nickel.

Socialism is no more an evil word than Christi-
anity. Socialism no more prescribed Joseph Stalin
and his secret police and shuttered churches than
Christianity prescribed the Spanish Inquisition.
Christianity and socialism alike, in fact, prescribe
a society dedicated to the proposition that all
men, women, and children are created equal, and
should not starve.

Adolf Hitler, incidentally, was a two-fer. He
named his party the National Socialists, the Nazis.
Hitler also had crosses painted on his tanks and
airplanes. The swastika wasn't a pagan symbol, as
so many people believe. It was a working person's
Christian cross, made of axes, of tools.

About Stalin's shuttered churches, and those
in China today: Such suppression of religion was

supposedly justified by Karl Marx's statement that "Religion is the opium of the people." Marx said that back in 1844, when opium and opium derivatives were the only effective pain killers anyone could take. Marx himself had taken them. He was grateful for the temporary relief they had given him. He was simply noticing, and surely not condemning, the fact that religion could also be comforting to those in economic or social distress. It was a casual truism, not a dictum.

When Marx wrote those words, by the way, we hadn't even freed our slaves yet. Whom do you imagine was more pleasing in the eyes of a merciful God back then? Karl Marx or the United States of America?

Stalin was happy to take Marx's truism as a decree, and Chinese tyrants as well, since it seemingly empowered them to put preachers out of business who might speak ill of them or their goals.

The statement has also entitled many in this country to say that socialists are anti-religion, are anti-God, and therefore absolutely loathsome.

I never met Carl Sandburg, and wish I had. I would have been tongue-tied in the presence of such

a national treasure. I did get to know one social-
ist of his generation, who was Powers Hapgood of
Indianapolis. After graduating from Harvard, he
went to work as a coal miner, urging his working-
class brothers to organize, in order to get better pay
and safer working conditions. He also led protesters
at the execution of the anarchists Nicolo Sacco and
Bartolomeo Vanzetti in Massachusetts in 1927.

Another of our freshwater ancestors was Eugene
Victor Debs, of Terre Haute, Indiana. A former
locomotive fireman, Eugene Debs ran for president
of the United States four times, the fourth time in
1920, when he was in prison. He said, "As long as
there is a lower class, I'm in it. As long as there is a
criminal element, I'm of it. As long as there's a soul
in prison, I am not free." Some platform.

A paraphrase of the Beatitudes.

And again: hooray for our team.

And our own beloved Carl Sandburg had this to
say about the fire-belching evangelist Billy Sunday:

You come along—tearing your shirt—yelling about Jesus.
I want to know what the hell you know about Jesus.

Jesus had a way of talking soft, and everybody except a few bankers and higher-ups among the con men of Jerusalem liked to have Jesus around because he never made any fake passes, and he helped the sick and gave people hope.

You come along calling us all damn fools—so fierce the froth of your own spit slobbers over your lips—always blabbering we're all going to hell straight off and you know all about it.

I've read Jesus's words. I know what he said. You don't throw any scare into me. I've got your number. I know how much you know about Jesus.

You tell people living in shanties Jesus is going to fix it up all right with them by giving them mansions in the skies after they're dead and the worms have eaten 'em.

You tell $6-a-week department store girls all they need is Jesus. You take a steel trust wop, dead without having lived, gray and shrunken at forty years of age, and you tell him to look at Jesus on the cross and he'll be all right.

You tell poor people they don't need any more money on pay day, and even if it's fierce to be out of a job, Jesus'll fix that all right, all right—all they gotta do is take Jesus the way you say.

Jesus played it different. The bankers and corporation lawyers of Jerusalem got their murderers to go after Jesus because Jesus wouldn't play their game.

I don't want a lot of gab from a bunkshooter in my religion.

Hooray for our team.

And I now take advantage of your hospitality by declaring myself a child of the Chicago Renaissance, powerfully humanized not only by Carl Sandburg, but by Edgar Lee Masters and Jane Addams and Louis Sullivan and Lake Michigan, and on and on.

And I propose a toast to an individual who wasn't an artist or working stiff of any description. She wasn't even a human being. Ladies and gentlemen of Chicago, I give you Mrs. O'Leary's cow.[7]

7 Mrs. O'Leary's cow is credited in folklore for kicking over a lantern in a barn and starting the Great Chicago Fire of 1871, which was followed by large-scale reconstruction that led to new economic and population growth.

15
HOW I GOT MY FIRST JOB
AS A REPORTER AND LEARNED TO
WRITE IN A SIMPLE, DIRECT WAY, WHILE
NOT GETTING A DEGREE IN ANTHROPOLOGY

From An Unsentimental Education: Writers and

Chicago, *University of Chicago Press, 1995*

"I'm not even sure what my message as a novelist is. But I would like to infect people with humane ideas before they're able to defend themselves."

I though a hell of a lot of the University of Chicago, and Chicago didn't think a damn thing about me. I was a very fringe character in the anthropology department.

Before Chicago, I had never been a liberal arts or social science major; I'd had chemistry at Cornell. And after Cornell, I was three years in the

goddamned infantry in World War II. That tore a
big chunk out of my life.

The University of Chicago gave returning
veterans a test on what they knew generally. They
took my credits, which were in physics, chemistry,
and math, and admitted me as a graduate student
in anthropology.

After going through the war and all, I thought
man was the thing to study. I really think it ought
to be done in second grade, but better in graduate
school than nowhere else. And it *was* interesting.

I had about three more years of credits from
Cornell, so I was one year short of a bachelor's.
But in the Hutchins system, a bachelor's degree
was given after two years, and I couldn't get
one.

And so, I had at least three years to go for a
master's. That was okay with me, because it was a
very exciting time in my life.

I was ready. I was like Thomas Wolfe when
he got to college, so excited that he was running
through the woods and jumping over stone walls
and barking like a dog.

Hell, I'd been an army private—I'd had a lousy

life for three years. So the university was sheer
luxury. The intellectual kick was great.

But I had a wife and kids, and I wrote a thesis
which was rejected by U of C. When I wasn't in
class, I was working as a reporter at the Chicago City
News Bureau. I also spent a lot of time with my fam-
ily, rather than at the university. I led a pretty separate
life, because I had a wife and kids. Most students
didn't. And in the summers, other people would go off
on digs or do fieldwork, but I couldn't. Because I had
a wife and kids, I had to keep working.

We had one superstar in the anthropology de-
partment, Robert Redfield. Victorian anthropology
had been completely discredited, because cultural
as well as physical evolution was assumed by the
Victorians: they believed that people progressed
from polygamy to monogamy, from many gods to
one, and so on. Redfield said, "Now, wait a minute:
there is one stage that every society goes through,
and I'll describe it." He called it the folk society.

The folk society was closed, isolated, from
outsiders. It included a common belief system and
extensive kinship relationships. It sounds comfort-
able, like what everybody's looking for.

I looked on the University of Chicago community as a folk society—and I felt like an outsider in it. I felt excluded by that bunch in the department, although they had admitted me. I wasn't treated badly, but they already *had* a family.

My ironic distance as a novelist has a lot to do with having been an anthropology student. Anthropology made me a cultural relativist, which is what everybody ought to be. People in the world over ought to be taught, seriously, that culture is a gadget, and that one culture is as arbitrary as another.

That's an important lesson, yet some people never hear of it. Then, when they're adult, they can't *bear* to hear of it.

Culture *is* a gadget; it's something we inherit. And you can fix it the way you fix a broken oil burner. You can fix it continuously.

❊

In my master's thesis, I studied what it takes to effect radical cultural change. What kind of a group do you need to put society through a 45-degree turn, or a 90-degree turn? It appeared that what you needed

was an authentic genius. Really, you need two very
bright guys who have status in the community.
One of them says, about the genius, "This guy is *not*
nuts." And then, you also need an explainer. For the
Cubists, there was Picasso, and there were Braque
and Apollinaire, who explained what they were
doing. (Picasso wasn't about to explain what the hell
he was doing. That would have been too tiresome.)

My thesis considered the Cubists and the Native
American ghost dance. An intensely bright profes-
sor named Sidney Slotkin worked with me on it.
Slotkin, too, was marginal in the anthropology
department, although he had come out of it; he
just wasn't their kind.

I studied how change can be made—but a
novelist can't make change. You can't. There's no
willpower. How dare somebody who is not a jour-
nalist or does not hold rank of some kind comment
on something as complicated as military logistics
or foreign policy or petroleum? Who the hell are
you? And you're gonna say what the government
should do next?

The novelist is in a funny position: utterly

unqualified. Having no badge or rank, and crack-
ing off about this or that. It peeves a lot of people.
How dare we do what we do?

Yet novelists can have a great effect on young
people. When I was between the ages of fourteen
and twenty and starting to read just about any-
thing, I had no immunity whatsoever to ideas. I
would read Hemingway, Steinbeck, Dos Passos,
and James T. Farrell—and their political opinions
would become mine.

I would assume that some kids have become
pacifists because of me. Actually, I'm not even
sure what my message as a novelist is. But I would
like to infect people with humane ideas before
they're able to defend themselves.

My boyhood dream was to cure cancer. Not
much chance of that. My brother was a scientist,
so I was going to be a scientist.

There were all these things I wanted to be, in-
stead of what I am.

My father had talked for a long time about my be-
coming an architect, but then he became filled with
self-pity and said, "Be anything but an architect."

If everything had gone right, right now I would
be an architect in Indianapolis. But instead I went
to Cornell to become a chemist.

And if everything had gone right in Chicago,
I would be a newspaper reporter or a managing
editor—or busting a strike!

The Chicago City News Bureau, where I
worked when I was in graduate school, was a
cocky operation. We were outlaws. It's where a
lot of journalists in Chicago start. The theory was
that working for City News was the only way
you'd be able to get a job on a Chicago newspaper.
You *had* to start there.

I could do at City News what I can't do right
now, which is walk into any part of town any-
where and start talking to people about their lives.

As a reporter, I'd go to police station after po-
lice station after police station, call on firehouses,
and then I'd go and call the coast guard: "Any-
thing going on?" For eight hours I'd be on the
South Side, the North Side, the West Side.

We were all looking around for everything.
Some of the reporters carried guns.

One time I found a body.

I started out as copyboy, just stuck there in the office, waiting for somebody to move on so I could become a reporter. One Sunday I was there and had the police radio on. I heard that in an office building three blocks over, a guy had just been killed in an elevator accident. There was nobody else to go, so I went over, and I got there as soon as the fire department and police did.

The top of the elevator had come down and crushed the elevator operator. And I got to see this guy squashed and dead.

I phoned the story in, and my editor said, "Okay, call up his wife. What does his wife say?"

I said, "I can't do that."

He said, "Yes, you can."

Oh it was so dishonorable! I wouldn't do it now. If I had worked at City News much longer, I probably would have gotten sick of it.

Still, being a journalist influenced me as a novelist. I mean, a lot of critics think I'm stupid because my sentences are so simple and my method is so direct: they think these are defects. No. The point is to write as much as you know as quickly as possible.

In journalism you learn to write a story so someone can cut it without even reading it, putting all the most important stuff in the beginning. And in my books, for the first few pages I say what the hell is going to happen. When I taught at the University of Iowa Writers' Workshop, I told my students, "Look, I want you to write in such a way that should you drop dead, the reader ought to be able to finish the story for you."

I wasn't writing fiction in Chicago, just news and anthropology papers. Later, I started writing short stories and selling them. So I said, Hey, I'm a writer, I guess!

When I left the university, there was a list of jobs open for anthropologists tacked on the department bulletin board. All of those jobs were for the PhDs, of course.

I got offered a job in public relations by General Electric and figured I'd better take it. I had a wife and kids, and just couldn't hold on any longer. So they hired me.

Particularly if you were a child of the Depression, in those days you just got a job. And you didn't feel destined for this or that job—you just got any goddamned job.

Later on, I was living on Cape Cod and needed to make a living. I wanted to teach high school, but I had no college degree. Since Chicago had turned down my thesis, I had about seven years of college and no degree.

So I wrote the people at Chicago a letter saying, "Hey, look, you guys, I'm way past a bachelor's. Won't you at least give me my bachelor's degree?"

And they said, "No. We're sorry, but you would have to come back here and take a course." It was Survey of Civilization, or something. There was no chance of my doing that; by then I had six kids.

So there I was, without any degree. Otherwise I would have become a teacher. I was quite angry about it.

I wrote *another* thesis, about the mathematical shapes of stories. That one was rejected too.

It got worse. Finally, I was on the faculty at Harvard, without a degree, and I had stopped bothering Chicago. I received a letter from a guy at Chicago who had taken over the division of social sciences.

He wrote, "I have just become dean of social sciences here, I was looking through a file, and I found an enormous envelope with your name on it. So I read it." And he added, "I am pleased to

tell you that under the rules of the university, you have always been entitled to a master's degree, for having published a book of quality."

Cat's Cradle is what qualified me for a master's degree.

That novel was anthropology, but *invented* anthropology: in it, I wrote about an invented society.

So I had been entitled to an MA all along. When my father was dying, he said, "I want to thank you, because you've never put a villain in any of your stories." The secret ingredient in my books is, there has never been a villain.

Some cultures we studied at Chicago were quite gruesome. The Aztecs were really scary, cutting people's hearts out. The Mayans weren't much better. And there have been instances of terrible cruelty even in benign societies, living in peace.

Society can be a villain, just the way a mother can be.

Yet it seems to me that it's no more trouble to be virtuous than to be vicious. I'm critical, but not a pessimist.

Look at all that humans can do! They're versatile. They can ride a unicycle. They can play the harp. They can, apparently, do *anything*.

Anyway, I liked the University of Chicago.
They didn't like *me*.

16
SOMEBODY SHOULD HAVE TOLD ME
NOT TO JOIN A FRATERNITY

"If I Knew Then What I Know Now: Advice to the Class of '94 from Those Who Know Best," Cornell Magazine, May 1994

Vonnegut thinks he'd have grown up faster if he'd hung out with the Independents instead of the frat boys. He also wishes someone would have told him that getting drunk was dangerous and stupid.

What I have become has almost nothing to do with Cornell, where, on the bad advice of my brother and father, I was attempting and failing to become a biochemist. It has everything to do with the absorbing adventure of writing for and editing *The Cornell Daily Sun*, a quite separate corporation.

Advice? Somebody should have told me not to

join a fraternity, but to hang out with the inde-
pendents, who were not then numerous. I would
have grown up faster that way. Somebody should
have told me that getting drunk, while fashion-
able, was dangerous and stupid. And somebody
should have told me to forget about higher educa-
tion, and to go to work for a newspaper instead.
That is what a lot of the most promising and
determined young writers used to do back then.
Nowadays, of course, you can't get a job at a
newspaper if you didn't have a college education.
Too bad.

My experiences at Cornell were freakish in
the extreme, as have been most of those which
followed, mostly accidents. So the advice I give
myself at the age of 71 is the best advice I could
have given myself in 1940, when detraining for the
first time in Ithaca, having come all the way from
Indianapolis: "Keep your hat on. We may wind up
miles from here."

17
THE MOST CENSORED WRITER OF HIS TIME
DEFENDS THE FIRST AMENDMENT

"The Idea Killers," Playboy Magazine, *January 1984*

Vonnegut observes that we have progressed from
the lynching of human beings to the lynching
of ideas, "which cannot scream in pain."

The American Civil Liberties Union, of which I
am an ardent supporter, has suggested that I may
be the most censored writer in America. I only
wish that my parents had lived to see that said
of me. My father's dying words were, "You will
never amount to a hill of beans." He didn't really
say that. I am making what we call a joke. Jokes
are protected by the First Amendment to our
Constitution. Even jokes about God Almighty.

Teachers and librarians have been unbelievably brave and honorable and patriotic, and also intelligent, during all the recent attacks on the First Amendment, which says, among other things, that all Americans are free to read or publish whatever they please. Slander and libel, of course, are excepted from the law's protection.

If I have been censored a lot, then teachers and librarians have had to defend my books a lot. I do not imagine for a microsecond that they have done that because what I write is so true and beautiful. Many of them may hate what I write, even though I am, at my worst, no more dangerous than a banana split. They defend my books, and anybody else's, because they are law-abiding and because they understand, as did our founding fathers, that it is vital in a democracy that voters have access to every sort of opinion and information.

Thanks to our founding fathers it is the law in this country that, once any idea is expressed here, no matter how repugnant it may be to some persons or, simply, to everybody, it must never be erased by the government. Even if the overwhelm-

ing majority of our people voted to have this or
that idea killed, the killing would be illegal be-
cause of the First Amendment, which says,

> "Article I—Congress shall make no law respect-
> ing an establishment of religion, or prohibiting the
> free exercise thereof; or abridging the freedom of
> speech or of the press; or the right of the people
> peaceably to assemble and to petition the govern-
> ment for a redress of grievances."

I am mainly concerned with freedom of speech
here, but that right is surely intertwined, as it is
in the First Amendment, with the separation of
church and state and the right to have our com-
plaints heard by our government.

*

Is there now a war about the First Amendment
going on in this unusually serene democracy of
ours? Well—an earlier draft of this essay was full
of warlike images. I am, after all, a war hero. I
allowed myself to be captured by the Germans
during World War Two in order to save lives.

In the warlike version—which, if read aloud, would sound a lot like the "1812" Overture—I had the teachers and the librarians draped over barbed wire, drowning in water-filled shell holes, and so on.

Concerned citizens such as you and I were in an officers' club in a bomb shelter 200 miles behind the lines. Up at the front, the censors and the book burners were wearing spiked helmets and using dumdums and mustard gas. They were yelling at the teachers and the librarians to surrender the First Amendment. The teachers and the librarians were yelling what General Anthony C. McAuliffe said to the Germans when they told him his situation was hopeless during the Battle of the Bulge. They were yelling, "Nuts! Nuts! Nuts!"

But the book burners and the censors are not, in fact, subhuman, maniacal, enemies. They are ordinary, usually likable, usually honorable neighbors of yours and mine. There is trouble between them and people like us, which often reaches courtrooms, because they believe, honestly, that they fully understand two sorts of laws that are supe-

rior to the Constitution: the laws of nature—and, above those, the laws of God.

To them, the hierarchy of laws is like a deck of playing cards. Laws made by God are aces. Laws made by nature are kings. Laws made by men are queens. The law against double parking would be the deuce of clubs, I suppose.

So when a censor sees or hears an idea that is being freely circulated in this democracy, an idea that tremendously offends him and probably a lot of other people, too, he tries to get rid of whatever is carrying that idea—a book, a magazine, a movie or whatever—by means of vigilante action or with the help of the government.

When somebody opposes him, saying that he is behaving in an unconstitutional manner, he replies that constitutional law is only a queen. He reaches into his pockets and pulls out four kings, natural laws that say that no real man will allow unpopular ideas to be expressed while he's around, and so on.

He lets that sink in, and then he pulls out four aces, which are God's laws. God Almighty Himself hates the idea that he wants squashed.

Does he win his case? Not in America. Maybe in
Iran he could, but he had better know his Koran.

In this country, we do not play with a full deck of
cards, which is what the censors find so hard to ac-
cept. We have agreed with one another, through the
instrument of our Constitution, that we will not,
when engaged in public business, behave as though
the laws of God and nature were fully understood.

This agreement is not some newfangled con-
traption that came in with rock 'n' roll and frontal
nudity. Censors commonly talk about getting back
to good old American fundamentals. How can they
disagree with us that, when we and they respect
the First Amendment, no matter how troubling that
amendment can be from time to time, we are being
as fundamentally American as we can get?

Perhaps the censors will agree with us, too, that
the most disgraceful episodes in our treatment of
human beings within our borders have taken place
when some people's idea of God's law or natural
law has been allowed to supersede our Constitu-
tion. I refer to human slavery, which so many
Americans believed to be natural and even or-

dained by God only the day before yesterday, in my
great-grandfather's time. it was finally the enforce-
ment of mere man's law that made slavery illegal.

During the first half of my own lifetime, lynch-
ings were shockingly common and always had
been. Not many people said that lynchings were in
accordance with God's law, but it seems likely that
a majority felt them to be in harmony with natural
law. What could be more natural, after all, than
that a community came to hate somebody so much
that its members strung him up or burned him
alive? (Castrating the offenders, incidentally, was
a natural preliminary to those natural rites. What
better way to protect the family?)

Fifty years ago, then, we might have been pro-
testing the lynchings of human beings. How much
less we have to complain of today—the lynchings
of mere ideas, which cannot scream in pain.

<p style="text-align:center">✳</p>

Still, the issue remains the same: Can the Constitu-
tion of the United States be made a scrap of paper
by appeals to what sincere persons believe the laws
of God and nature to be? If we let that happen, I

see no reason why we can't get back to the good old American practices of lynchings and even slavery again. What better way to fight crime?

If we did get back to slavery, then ideas might truly become dangerous, which they are not now. Just imagine what slaves might do if they got hold of a copy of the Constitution, for instance, and learned that all people, regardless of their opinions or their color or whatever, should be allowed to say whatever they like and to otherwise be free and equal.

I have alluded to the pain, the screams emitted by a lynched person. I will mention pain yet again. It is very often real pain that censors feel when they see this idea or that one, this image or that one, freely circulated for all to contemplate. I myself often feel that pain. New York's Forty-second Street makes me want to die. There can't be many thoughtful Americans who were not sickened by the beliefs that the American Nazi Party proposed to celebrate in Skokie, Illinois, a few years ago. We endured that Skokie pain in order that we ourselves might have the right to speak our minds, no matter how unpopular some of our views might be.

Our founding fathers never promised us that this would be a painless form of Government, that adhering to the Bill of Rights would invariably be delightful. Nor are Americans proud of avoiding pain at all costs. On patriotic holidays, in fact, we boast of how much pain Americans have stood in order to protect their freedoms—draped over barbed wire, drowning in water-filled shell holes, and so on.

So it is not too much to ask of Americans that they not be censors, that they run the risk of being deeply wounded by ideas so that we may all be free. If we are wounded by an ugly idea, we must count it as part of the cost of freedom and, like American heroes in the days gone by, bravely carry on.

18
MY DOG LIKES EVERYBODY, BUT WAS NOT INSPIRED BY ANCIENT GREECE AND ROME OR THE RENAISSANCE

"Why My Dog Is Not a Humanist," The Humanist,
November/December 1992

The Humanist of the Year finds that Science is yet another human-made God, to which he need not genuflect— nor does his dog, Sandy, who likes people.

I was once a Boy Scout. The motto of the Boy Scouts, as you know, is "Be Prepared." So, several years ago I wrote a speech to be delivered in the event that I won the Nobel Prize for Literature.

It was only eight words long. I think I had better use it here. (Use it or lose it, as the saying goes.)

This is it: "You have made me an old, old man."

❊

I think I got this great honor because I've lasted
so long. I dare to say of Humanism what Lyndon
Johnson said of politics. He said, "Politics ain't
hard. You just hang around and go to funerals."

Forgive me if I am not solemn about my award
tonight. I am here for your companionship and not
any award.

Nicholas Murray Butler, the late president of
Columbia University, was said by H. L. Mencken
to have received more honorary degrees and med-
als and citations and so on than anyone else then on
the planet. Mencken declared that all that remained
to be done for him was to wrap him in sheet gold
and burnish him until he blinded the sun itself.

❊

This is not the first time I have been accused of be-
ing a humanist. All of twenty-five years ago, when I
was teaching at the University of Iowa, a student all
of a sudden said to me, "I hear you're a Humanist."

I said, "Oh, yeah? What's a Humanist?"

He said, "That's what I'm asking you. Aren't
you getting paid to answer questions like that?"

I pointed out that my salary was a very modest one.

I then gave him the names of several full professors
who were making a heck of a lot more money than I
was and who were doctors of philosophy besides—
which I sure as heck wasn't, and which I am not now.

<p style="text-align:center">✻</p>

But his accusation stuck in my craw. And in the pro-
cess of trying to cough it up so I could look at it, it
occurred to me that a humanist, perhaps, was some-
body who was crazy about human beings, who, like
Will Rogers, had never met one he didn't like.

That certainly did not describe me.

It did describe my dog, though. His name was
Sandy, although he wasn't a Scotsman. He was
a puli—a Hungarian sheepdog with a face full of
hair. I am a German, with a face full of hair.

I took Sandy to the little zoo in Iowa City. I expect-
ed him to enjoy the buffalo and the prairie dogs and
the raccoons and the possums and the foxes and the
wolves and so on, and especially their stinks, which in
the case of the buffalo were absolutely overwhelming.

But all Sandy paid any attention to was people,
his tail wagging all the time. What a person
looked like or smelled like didn't matter to Sandy.
It could be a baby. It could be a drunk who hated

dogs. It could be a young woman as voluptuous as Marilyn Monroe. It could have been Hitler. It could have been Eleanor Roosevelt. Whoever it was, Sandy would have wagged his tail.

I disqualified him as a humanist, though, after reading in the *Encyclopedia Britannica* that humanists were inspired by ancient Greece and Rome at their most rational, and by the Renaissance. No dog, not even Rin Tin Tin or Lassie, has ever been that. Humanists, moreover, I learned, were strikingly secular in their interests and enthusiasms, did not try to factor God Almighty into their equations, so to speak, along with all that could be seen and heard and felt and smelled and tasted in the here and now. Sandy obviously worshipped not just me but simply any person as though he or she were the creator and manager of the universe.

He was simply too dumb to be a humanist.

※

Sir Isaac Newton, incidentally, did think that was a reasonable thing to do—to factor in a conventional God Almighty, along with whatever else might be going on. I don't believe Benjamin

Franklin ever did. Charles Darwin pretended to
do that, because of his place in polite society. But
he was obviously very happy, after his visit to the
Galapagos Islands, to give up that pretense. That
was only 150 years ago.

※

As long as I've mentioned Franklin, let me digress
a moment. He was a Freemason, as were Voltaire
and Frederick the Great, and so were Washington
and Jefferson and Madison.

Most of us here, I guess, would be honored if it
was said that such great human beings were our
spiritual ancestors. So why isn't this a gathering of
Freemasons?

Can somebody here, after this speech, if you don't
mind, tell me what went wrong with Freemasonry?

※

This much I think I understand: in Franklin's
time—and in Voltaire's—Freemasonry was per-
ceived as being anti-Catholic. To be a Freemason
was cause for excommunication from the Roman
Catholic Church.

As the Roman Catholic population of this coun-
try grew by leaps and bounds, to be anti-Catholic—

in New York and Chicago and Boston, at least—
was political suicide. It was also business suicide.

※

None of my real ancestors, blood ancestors, ge-
netic ancestors in this country—every one of them
of German descent—was a Freemason, so far as I
know, and I am the fourth generation Vonnegut to
be born here. Before World War I, though, a lot of
them took part in the activities of a highly respect-
able but not impossibly serious organization much
like this one, which they called "the Freethinkers."

There are a few Americans who call themselves
that still—some of you in this room, no doubt. But
the Freethinkers no longer exist as an organized
presence of which communities are aware. This
is because the movement was so overwhelmingly
German American, and most German Americans
found it prudent to abandon all activities that
might make them seem apart from the general
population when we entered World War I. Many
Freethinkers, incidentally, were German Jews.

※

My great-grandfather Clemens Vonnegut, an im-
migrant merchant from Munster, became a Free-

thinker after reading Darwin. In Indianapolis,
there is a public school named after him. He was
head of the school board there for many years.

So the sort of Humanism I represent, to which
I am an heir, draws energy not from the Renais-
sance or from an idealized pre-Christian Greece
and Rome but, rather, from very recent scientific
discoveries and modes of seeking truth.

I myself at one time tried to become a biochem-
ist—as did our darling, terribly missed brother
Isaac Asimov. He actually became one. I didn't
have a chance. He was smarter than me. We both
knew that, incidentally. He is in heaven now.

My paternal grandfather and father were both
architects, restructuring the reality of India-
napolis with meticulously measured quantities of
materials whose presence—unlike that of a con-
ventional God Almighty—could not be doubted:
wood and steel, sand and lime and stone, copper,
brass, bricks.

My only surviving sibling, Dr. Bernard Von-
negut, eight years my senior, is a physical chemist
who thinks and thinks about the distribution of
electrical charges in thunderstorms.

❈

But now my big brother, like Isaac Asimov near the end of his life, surely, and like most of us here, has to admit that the fruits of science so far, put into the hands of governments, have turned out to be cruelties and stupidities exceeding by far those of the Spanish Inquisition and Genghis Khan and Ivan the Terrible and most of the demented Roman emperors, not excepting Heliogabalus.

Heliogabalus had a hollow iron bull in his banquet hall that had a door in its side. Its mouth was a hole, so sound could get out. He would have a human being put inside the bull and then a fire built on a hearth under its belly, so that the guests at his banquets would be entertained by the noises the bull made.

❈

We modern humans roast people alive, tear their arms and legs off, or whatever, using airplanes or missile launchers or ships or artillery batteries— and do not hear their screams.

When I was a little boy in Indianapolis, I used to be thankful that there were no longer torture

chambers with iron maidens and racks and thumb-
screws and Spanish boots and so on. But there may
be more of them now than ever—not in this coun-
try but elsewhere, often in countries we call our
friends. Ask Human Rights Watch. Ask Amnesty
International if this isn't so. Don't ask the U.S.
State Department.

And the horrors of those torture chambers—their
powers of persuasion—have been upgraded, like
those of warfare, by applied science, by the domes-
tication of electricity and the detailed understand-
ing of the human nervous system, and so on.

❉

Napalm, incidentally, is a gift to civilization from
the chemistry department of Harvard University.

❉

So science is yet another human-made God to
which I, unless in a satirical mood, an ironical
mood, a lampooning mood, need not genuflect.

UNSTUCK IN TIME—QUOTES TO PONDER

"Keep your hat on.
We may end up miles from here!"

❊

"Practicing an art, no matter how well or badly,
is a way to make your soul grow, for heaven's
sake. Sing in the shower. Dance to the radio.
Tell stories."

❊

"True terror is to wake up one morning
and discover that your high school class
is running the country."

❊

"A purpose of human life, no matter
who is controlling it, is to love whoever is
around to be loved."

❊

"My father was a gun nut, like Ernest
Hemingway, mainly to prove that he wasn't
effeminate, even though he was an architect and
a painter. He didn't get drunk and slug people.
Shooting animals was enough."

❊

"The good earth—we could have saved it, but
we were too damn cheap and lazy."

❊

"We have to be constantly jumping
off cliffs and developing our wings
on the way down."

❊

"You're learning that you do not inhabit
a solid, reliable social structure—that the older
people around you are worried, moody, goofy
human beings who themselves were little kids
only a few days ago. So homes can fall
apart and schools can fall apart, usually
for childish reasons . . ."

❊

"Those who believe in telekinetics,
raise my hand."

✻

"When things go well for days on end,
it is a hilarious accident."

✻

"Make love when you can.
It's good for you."

✻

"Male American artists don't even have to
shoot off guns anymore. They can even be
homosexuals, and the hell with it.
This is good."

✻

"Queer travel suggestions are
dancing lessons from God."

✻

"Humanists try to behave decently and hon-
orably without any expectation of rewards or
punishments in an afterlife. And since the cre-
ator of the universe is unknowable to us so far,
we serve as best we can the highest abstraction
of which we have some understanding, which
is our community."

✻

"Another flaw in the human character is
that everybody wants to build and nobody
wants to maintain it."

❊

"Write a poem to a friend, even a lousy poem.
Do it as well as you possibly can. You will
get an enormous reward. You will have
created something."

❊

"There is only one rule that I know of, babies—,
Goddamn it, you've got to be kind."

❊

"I am enchanted by the Sermon on the Mount.
Being merciful, it seems to me, is the only good
idea we have received so far. Perhaps we will
get another good idea by and by—and then we
will have two good ideas."

❊

"A sane person in an insane society
must appear insane."

❊

"It is true that some of the characters speak coarsely. That is because people speak coarsely in real life. Especially soldiers and hardworking men speak coarsely, and even our most sheltered children know that. And we all know, too, that those words really don't damage children much. They didn't damage us when we were young. It was evil deeds and lying that hurt us."

❊

"Dear future generations:
Please accept our apologies.
We were roaring drunk on petroleum."

❊

"We have mortally wounded this sweet life-supporting planet—the only one in the whole Milky Way—with a century of transportation whoopee. Our government is conducting a war on drugs, is it? Let them go after petroleum! Talk about a destructive high! You put some of this stuff in your car and you can go a hundred miles an hour, run over the neighbor's dog, and tear the atmosphere to smithereens."

❊

"We are dancing animals."

❋

"Hopelessness is the mother
of originality."

❋

"Librarians, not famous for their physical
strength or their powerful political connections or
their great wealth, who, all over this country, have
staunchly resisted anti-democratic bullies who
have tried to remove certain books from
their shelves, and have refused to reveal to thought
police the names of persons who
have checked out those titles."

❋

"I was a victim of a series
of accidents, as are we all."

❋

"I'm a space wanderer named Kurt."

❋

"So it goes . . ."

❋

ETC.